php|architect's Guide to PHP Development in the Cloud

by Ivo Jansch and Vito Chin

BLUE PARABOLA

PHP Development in the Cloud - a php|architect Guide

Contents Copyright ©2010–2011 Ivo Jansch and Brain Chin Vito – All Rights Reserved
Book and cover layout, design and text Copyright ©2004-2011 Blue Parabola, LLC. and its predecessors – All Rights Reserved

First Edition: February 2011
ISBN: **978-0-9810345-2-2**
Produced in Canada
Printed in the United States

No part of this book may be reproduced, stored in a retrieval system, or transmitted in any form or by means without the prior written permission of the publisher, except in the case of brief quotations embedded in critical reviews or articles.

Disclaimer

Although every effort has been made in the preparation of this book to ensure the accuracy of the information contained therein, this book is provided "as-is" and the publisher, the author(s), their distributors and retailers, as well as all affiliated, related or subsidiary parties take no responsibility for any inaccuracy and any and all damages caused, either directly or indirectly, by the use of such information. We have endeavored to properly provide trademark information on all companies and products mentioned in the book by the appropriate use of capitals. However, we cannot guarantee the accuracy of such information.

Blue Parabola, The Blue Parabola logo, php|architect, the php|architect logo, NanoBook and the NanoBook logo are trademarks or registered trademarks of Blue Parabola, LLC, its assigns, partners, predecessors and successors.

Written by	Ivo Jansch and Vito Chin
Published by	Blue Parabola, LLC.
	28 Bombay Ave.
	Toronto, ON M3H 1B7
	Canada
	(416) 630-6202 / (877) 630-6202
	info@phparch.com / www.phparch.com
Publisher	Marco Tabini
Technical Reviewer	Koen van Urk
Copy Editor	Stan Tymorek
Layout and Design	Arbi Arzoumani
Managing Editor	Elizabeth Tucker Long
Finance and Resource Management	Emanuela Corso

Contents

Acknowledgements   **xi**
    A Few Words From Vito xi
    A Few Words From Ivo xii

Foreword   **xv**

Chapter 1 — Introduction   **1**
    The Book's Structure 1
    The Sample Code Application: PictureMe 2
    Conventions 3
    Staying Up-to-date 3

Chapter 2 — Cloud Computing Primer   **5**
    What is Cloud Computing? 5
        Five Essential Characteristics 6
        Three Service Models 7
        Four Deployment Models 8
    Current State of Affairs 9
        Technology Trigger 10
        The Peak of Inflated Expectations 10
        Trough of Disillusionment 11
        Slope of Enlightenment 11
        Plateau of Productivity 11
    Infrastructure as a Service 12

Platform as a Service 13
Software as a Service 14

Chapter 3 — Cloud Basics   19
General Prerequisites 19
    PHP 19
    Object-Oriented Development 20
    Network Programming 20
    XML 22
    JSON 23
Virtualization 24
Clustering 25
Web Services 26
    SOAP 26
    REST 27
    HTTP APIs 28
System Administration 29

Chapter 4 — Cloud Architecture   31
Horizontal Scalability 31
    Load-balancing 34
    Parallel Distributed Job Processing 36
    Sessions 36
    Distributed File-storage 37
    Automatic Deployment 38
    Creating a Package for the Package Manager 40
    Creating a Repository 42
    Installing an Application From a Package on a Cloud Instance 43
Bottleneck Prevention 44
    Types of Bottlenecks 45
    Using Xdebug Profiler to Identify Bottlenecks 46
    Circumventing Bottlenecks with the Cloud 48
Abstraction 49
Multi-Tenancy 51
    Separate Applications, Separate Databases 52

One Application, Separate Databases	52
Separate Applications, One Database	52
One Application, One Database	52
Advanced Approaches	53

Chapter 5 — Working with Popular Cloud Infrastructures — 55

Amazon's Cloud	55
Amazon's S3, CloudFront, EC2 and Elastic MapReduce	56
PictureMe: the Cloud Application	57
Requirements	57
Storing Pictures in S3	58
Geographical Optimization with CloudFront	60
Amazon's Elastic Compute Cloud	61
Searching for Colors	63
MapReduce	65
Hadoop's Map Reduce	66
The Color Indexing Architecture	66
The Color Grid	67
The Mapper	70
The Reducer	71
Sandboxing on a VM with Apache Hadoop	72
Creating the JobFlow on Elastic MapReduce	74
Updating the Color Index to Local Storage	75
Tokyo Cabinet and Tokyo Tyrant	75
tokyo_tyrant Extension	75
Handling Search Requests	77
Mapping Matching Positions	79
Automatic Elasticity with Rackspace Cloud	80
The Rackspace Cloud	81
Distributed Processing for PictureMe	82
Tackling the Bottleneck: _putColorGrid of PictureManager	84
WorkerManager	85
Spawning Workers	86
The Worker	87

viii ■ CONTENTS

        Monitoring Workers 89
        Monitoring Worker Servers 91
        Starting Up a New Worker Server 92
        Stopping a Worker Server 93
        The Worker Server Image 94
        Authentication 95
        Conclusion 96
    Microsoft's Azure Cloud 96
        Windows Azure 96
        SQL Azure 100
        AppFabric (Formerly Known as .NET Services) 100

Chapter 6 — Working with Popular Cloud Platforms   **103**
    Google App Engine 103
        App Engine and PHP 104
        A Look at Quercus 105
        Getting PHP Apps Running in App Engine through Quercus 107
        Administration and Monitoring 112
    Rackspace Cloud Sites 112
    Other Platforms 114

Chapter 7 — Working with Popular Cloud Software and Services   **117**
    Identification Using OpenID 117
        Login Request 119
        Identity Provider Authorization 120
        Verification 121
    Authorization Using OAuth 122
        Registering with the Service Provider 123
        Getting a Request Token 123
        Getting an Access Token 125
        Fetching Resources 126
    Search 127
        Google Search 127
        Twitter Search 130
    Payments 132

Google Checkout	132
Google Checkout APIs	133
Paypal	135
CRM	136
Making Salesforce Easier with PHP	138
Connecting and Logging on to Salesforce.com	138
Listing Profiles	140
Creating a User	140
Disabling a User	141
Listing Users	141
Upserting a User	142
Creating an Authentication Web Service	142
Enabling Single Sign-On on Salesforce.com	143
Access Salesforce.com Seamlessly from your Local Server	144
Conclusion	145
Maps	145
Google Maps with PHP	145
Storage	147
Scalability	149
Performance	149
Object Size	149
Download Options	149
Security	149
Regional Optimization and Flexibility	150
Reliability	150
Cost-Efficiency	150
Amazon Simple Storage Service (S3)	150
Rackspace Cloud Files	151
Nirvanix Storage Delivery Network	151
The Planet's Storage Cloud	151
EMC Atmos Online Storage Service	151
Conclusion	151

Acknowledgements

A Few Words From Vito

Some say the Sixties were a hugely influential decade. It was an era of liberation, revolution and technological advancement. I wasn't born in the Sixties. What I know of the Sixties, I learned from listening to stories from people that had lived during that decade, and from books, music and movies. On the software front, an entire model of cooperative software development that had shaped the cloud as it is today had its roots in the social and political movement of the Sixties.

If the Sixties gave us the spirit, the Noughties was about practical commercialization, even within a free-spirited context.

I once had a dog named Bobo who was never leashed. We once brought Bobo along on a mountain hiking trip about three miles from our house. He wandered off as we were trekking and somehow got lost in the woods. We tried to locate him when we realized he was lost (he usually just hangs about and catch up with us) but to no avail. So, we gave up and went home. About two days later, there he was lying down on the porch, looking exhausted but still as cheerful as ever.

While the Sixties instilled upon my family the idea that Bobo should roam free, the Noughties saw the introduction of functional products such as GPS dog collars and Cloud-based maps to allow us to locate Bobo. We did not have GPS collars back when Bobo got lost, because that was in the Nineties; but Bobo of the Noughties could had been spared the two days of wandering and sniffing about to find his way home. But then, he'd have missed all of the adventure.

The moral of the story is freedom. Not freedom to roam, but freedom of choice and possibilities. As you read this book, you'll find that many services that had marketed themselves as being cloud-based offer such freedom of choice, and more. You could choose to use a GPS dog collar on your dog and worry less, or choose not to worry at all in the first place, just as you can choose to have that automatically scalable PaaS or think about scaling only when you need to. It all depends on what you want.

This book is about the cloud. The cloud is a metaphor, an idealization if you will, of the congregation of technologies and philosophies that was forged by the ideologies of the Sixties and made real by the commercial abilities of the Noughties. To the people who made a positive difference in these decades, I owe them my gratitude.

And of course, to my family, friends, colleagues and Ivo, my co-author: thank you.

A Few Words From Ivo

One of my favorite movies is The Matrix. The concept of a virtual reality that goes as far as to provide our brains with sensory inputs is so intriguing that a few years ago I created the website Simulism.org to explore the possibilities of virtual worlds and simulations of the universe. Cloud computing is a technology that has a lot of similarities to The Matrix; it is all about virtualization of resources. Applications are run on a cloud thinking they are run on physical hardware and have no idea that they are running on virtual hardware. You could say that The Cloud is to applications what The Matrix is to humans.

Not in the least because of this intriguing aspect, I have found it enjoyable to explore the possibilities of what cloud computing can offer us. While writing this book I got a really good sense of what the future of computing might look like. I hope that like Vito and me, you will become enthusiastic about cloud computing by reading about the possibilities it offers you.

I would like to thank Vito, who did the majority of the work to get this book published, and Elizabeth Tucker Long, our coach at php|architect, for keeping an eye on our work and chasing us when we needed to hit deadlines; persistent but never unpleasant.

And my 93-year-old grandmother, for simply saying, "I have no clue what you're writing about, but I want a copy!" and of course Leoni, for enduring the hours of solitude while I was busy getting this book out.

To all who have inspired this book in one way or another: thanks!

Foreword

These days, no good IT proposal or whitepaper is complete without a section on "the cloud." The cloud has become so ubiquitous in IT speak that it has actually come to represent a whole host of services ranging from Software as a Service to Infrastructure as a Service. The former has been an understood pattern for a long time in IT, while the latter is a relative newcomer. When discussing cloud services, there are a variety of types of clouds ranging from Virtual Private Servers to truly amorphous infrastructures, like Google's App Engine and Microsoft's Azure. Truly, as we begin to inspect the cloud, we begin to see that it is not a single thunderstorm but many localized storms that each serves a unique purpose.

IT managers have to tread carefully; where there are clouds, there are usually slippery surfaces that can quickly put a good project into a tailspin. Reaching into the cloud for solutions may seem like a good idea at the time. In many cases, pushing your application into a respectable cloud run by a reputable vendor can help you stay safely on course, but even this path is difficult to follow and managers should proceed with caution.

When pushing to the cloud, a manager is committing his or her application to that vendor's infrastructure. Since most vendors have unique API signatures, committing to this vendor lock-in is akin to building a cloud city. These "cloud cities" can see their infrastructure quickly evaporate and their foundation blow away as vendors disappear or change strategies.

It is into this confusion of low-hanging buzzwords and bad puns that swirl around an IT manager's head, creating confusion and obscuring true solutions - more of a fog than a cloud - that Ivo and Vito venture.

It was my great pleasure, for the majority of 2009, to live in the Netherlands and work with Ivo at Ibuildings before he moved on to found Egeniq. One of the fun things about working with Ivo is arguing with him. It is my firm belief that Ivo will strike a contrary position, just to spark an argument. However, each time he and I engaged in a battle of wits (we did not keep score but I firmly believe I won more than he did), I came out the wiser. Regardless of his position, Ivo would present his case with passion and conviction. This passion carries over into his writing. I have full confidence that this book will help you clear the fog surrounding the cloud options you are considering and lead you to the proper solution at the end of the rainbow.

While at Ibuildings, I also worked with Vito on several projects, most revolving around techPortal, Ibuildings' tutorial blog or the Dutch PHP Conference. In every contact I had with him, I came away impressed by not only his knowledge of his subject matter, but his passion for sharing. I feel that there is no greater attribute a developer can have than passion. Vito obviously loves working with code and more importantly, sharing what he knows with others.

Cal Evans
CMO of Blue Parabola

Chapter 1

Introduction

This book is the result of two people's interest in both PHP and cloud computing. It explains to PHP developers what they need to know to not only understand the cloud concept, but to be able to put it to good use. To accomplish this, we mix explanations of cloud concepts with practical examples. All of the code snippets in this book are examples of real-life scenarios. We hope that they provide you with a basis to start from when you venture into cloud computing, or at least give you an impression of what coding in the cloud typically means.

The Book's Structure

We have structured the book in such a way that you can either read it front to back, or dive into one of the chapters based on a particular interest. We have tried to arrange the chapters in such a way that they also provide a path from the more easy concepts to the more complex and abstract ones.

Here is a short overview of each of the chapters:

Chapter 1 is the general introduction to the book. You can safely skip this and not miss out on anything. On the other hand, if you're reading this, you've already covered most of the introduction so it's not written entirely in vain.

Chapter 2 contains a cloud-computing primer. For developers new to the concept of cloud computing it provides an introduction to the concept. For developers familiar with the concept it provides our vision of cloud computing, so it's clear to the reader what we as the authors think are the essential characteristics of cloud technology.

Chapter 3 explains the basics every developer should know when dealing with cloud computing. It explains the basic technologies underlying clouds, and explains what skills PHP developers should try to learn in order to meet a set of prerequisites for dealing with the cloud.

Chapter 4 takes that to the next level: it explains from an application architecture point of view what developers must know to make their applications "cloud ready." There are a number of concepts that you can introduce into the architecture of an application even before you run it on a cloud. These concepts make the application more scalable, and allow you to effectively deploy the application to a cloud environment.

Chapters 5 through 7 take you through a number of practical examples, working with cloud technology in a very hands-on way. We show you the PHP code you need to write, and the steps you need to take to deploy an application to the cloud; in other words, this is the part where we actually teach you the ins and outs of working with clouds.

The Sample Code Application: PictureMe

Most code samples within this book are within the context of the PictureMe application: a small image manager that allows end-users to upload, list, view and delete pictures. It also highlights some techniques used for color-searching, identification, mapping, etc., which you'll see later in this book.

We try to be as minimal as possible when creating this application as its purpose is to complement the discussion in the book. It is designed to be readable. In fact, we think you'll do quite well reading the code from start to end if you begin with `index.php`.

The code is framework-neutral and has no specific fidelity to any library. Some libraries or parts-of frameworks are included. Though for convenience if you wish to try them out within the scope of a feature for PictureMe, `config.inc.php` will allow you to peruse and change the range of options available as you explore the book and the cloud. Sample code[1] is available for downloaded as well.

Conventions

Throughout the book, we use a number of conventions in our examples. The most important one is the way we denote placeholders in square-brackets. For example,

```
# scp -i [private_key_file] root@[hostname]:/var/www/html/
```

In the example above, *private_key_file* and *hostname* are placeholders. Placeholders are indications where you should place your own value. We mostly use example values instead of placeholders, but will use placeholders where we think it will be more convenient for you to know where your own values will be required.

Staying Up-to-date

Keep an eye on the book's companion website[2]. We will post any updates to the book or errata on this site. Also, you may want to follow us on twitter: @vitoc and @ijansch; we tweet about many different subjects but PHP is a major one for both of us.

---

[1] http://cloudphp.net/download
[2] http://cloudphp.net//

Chapter 2

Cloud Computing Primer

What is Cloud Computing?

Before we start with the first examples, we first need to define what cloud computing really is and what it is not, so that we can get a clear picture of what we are going to cover in this book. There's been a lot of talk about clouds the past few years; it's essentially turned into hype. Is it the solution that will magically solve all our current hosting problems? Is it just a set of empty promises? Is it just a new terminology for something that we've been doing for years?

Let's see if we can give a concrete definition of the cloud. One of the most pragmatic explanations of cloud computing is the one used by the National Institute of Standards and Technology (NIST)[1]. We love it so much that we suggest that this definition be adopted by the PHP community, so we'll use this as our definition throughout the book. NIST[2] describes the cloud as follows:

---

[1] http:\//csrc.nist.gov/groups/SNS/cloud-computing/
[2] The National Institute of Standards and Technology's description of Cloud Computing, v15 (July 10, 2009)

6 ■ Cloud Computing Primer

> "Cloud computing is a model for enabling convenient, on-demand network access to a shared pool of configurable computing resources (e.g., networks, servers, storage, applications, and services) that can be rapidly provisioned and released with minimal management effort or service provider interaction. This cloud model promotes availability and is composed of five essential **characteristics**, three **service models**, and four **deployment models**."

That's a mouthful. To make this description less academic, we should look at the characteristics, service models and deployment models mentioned.

Five Essential Characteristics

NIST lists the following characteristics as something that considers itself 'cloud' should have. We'll list them below along with a bit of explanation.

With **On-demand, Self-service**, the NIST suggests that people should be able to use cloud services when they need them, without intervention by people. If we use Microsoft Azure Storage services as an example of cloud storage, we can indeed see that we can use storage whenever we need it, and we can grow and shrink our storage without having to talk to a salesperson.

Broad network access means that typical cloud services are accessible over the Internet or at least an internal network. You might say that anything connected to the Internet has this characteristic, but cloud computing is about the combination of characteristics, so don't give up on it just yet.

Resource pooling is an important concept that we'll dive into in more detail later in this book. What it basically means is that instead of everyone using their own resources, resources are pooled so they can be used more efficiently. One of the pioneers of cloud computing, Amazon, started their S3 storage service and EC2 virtual hosting platform because they had spare capacity on their server infrastructure that they wanted to put to good use. Instead of requiring people to buy their own hardware, Amazon lets you use their hardware. Resource pooling is cost efficient, but also considered 'green', as there is a lot less wasted computing capacity in cloud environments.

Rapid elasticity means that cloud services should be able to help you scale up and down as needed. Later in this book we will look at as an example of a cloud application that is elastic. Whether you have one user with 10 customers in total or 130 users with hundreds of thousands of customers, you don't notice any difference in the user experience. Salesforce's platform scales up and down as needed to accommodate small and large situations.

Measured Service means that instead of paying fixed license fees, cloud services typically have a business model that is based on actual use. This is very similar to how we deal with our electricity bills. We use a certain amount of energy, and that's what we pay for. Cloud services typically use the same model. Whether paying per megabyte for a storage service or paying per user in an environment such as Salesforce, we pay less if we use less and more if we use more.

These are the five major characteristics NIST proposes. Something that is supposed to be "cloud," should display at least a number of these characteristics.

Three Service Models

NIST also proposes three distinct service models. They are well-chosen because all cloud services fit into one of the three models. On the other hand, however, it's often not easy to determine which model a service belongs to. The three models are:

Infrastructure as a Service (IaaS) is a category of services deals with providing infrastructure components. Think of storage that is offered as a service, virtual machine instances, memory, resources; basically everything that you normally use when building your own hardware infrastructure can be offered as a service so you don't have to worry about hardware.

In **Platform as a Service (PaaS)** model, the whole platform is offered as a single service, instead of offering each of the infrastructure components separately. In a Platform as a Service offering, an application does not need to know anything about the underlying hardware infrastructure. Whether it's running on one machine or 100, or whether it's using one hard disk or 20, with Platform as a Service this is abstracted away from us. The application runs as if it were on a single machine, using a single hard disk for storage. The Platform as a Service offering takes care of the details.

With **Software as a Service (SaaS)**, we don't care about the hosting at all, because we're now dealing with applications and application components that work out of the box. We don't have to worry how or where the application is hosted. We just know that it works and that we can use it, and ideally talk to it from our own applications.

It is our opinion that out of the five characteristics, the three service models and the four deployment models, the service models are the most practical way to classify cloud services. So we will look at the three service models in more detail later in this chapter. On top of that we've made the service models a key element of the structure of this book: Chapters 5 through 7 each dive into one of the three service models.

Four Deployment Models

The final part of NIST's cloud definition looks at how clouds are generally deployed. The four ways to deploy cloud applications are:

Private Clouds are clouds that are accessible only within an organization. They can be hosted on-premise or offsite, but access is restricted. This is useful if you want to be in full control of the cloud. It's not only cool to say "we have our own cloud," it gives you more control over the cloud, which is useful from both a flexibility, security and performance perspective. A slight disadvantage might be that resource pooling would be only done among your own resources, but for many applications this is acceptable.

Public Clouds are cloud services that are accessible to anyone. Amazon's S3 cloud-storage service provides storage to anyone who needs it. Resource pooling is generally done across all users, making it a very flexible system.

A **Community Cloud** is more or less in between a private and a public cloud; services are accessible to members within a certain community. Google App Engine is an example of a cloud platform that is predominantly useful to the Python and Java communities.

Some things just don't like to be put in a specific category, so NIST accommodated a **Hybrid Cloud** category for those services that employ characteristics from any of the above categories. Companies that use a combination of private and public cloud services are considered to operate a "hybrid cloud."

The deployment models are a weaker part of the definition, as this division can be applied to virtually anything based on who has access to something. However, since we use the NIST definition as our standard, the book wouldn't be complete without mentioning the deployment models.

Current State of Affairs

So now we have more or less an idea of what cloud computing means. (OK, admittedly we still only have looked at abstract concepts so far, but throughout the book we'll make these more concrete.) Let's look at the current state of cloud computing. We hope this book will be relatively timeless so by the time you read this things might have changed, but at the time of writing we can say that cloud computing is, as Gartner calls it, at the "peak of inflated expectations." Gartner, the renowned IT analyst company, uses their so-called 'Hype Cycle' (see Figure 2.2) to investigate the state of technologies. In 2009, they looked at cloud computing[3] and positioned it in their hype cycle (See Figure 2.2).

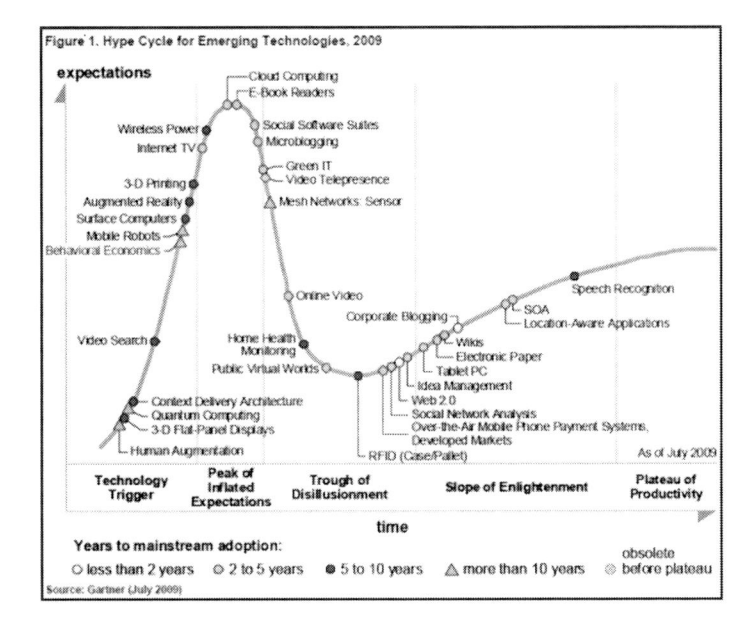

Figure 2.1

The hype cycle differentiates four states that every major technology goes through. Let's look at where cloud computing fits according to Gartner and according to us.

---
[3]http://www.gartner.com/it/page.jsp?id=1124212

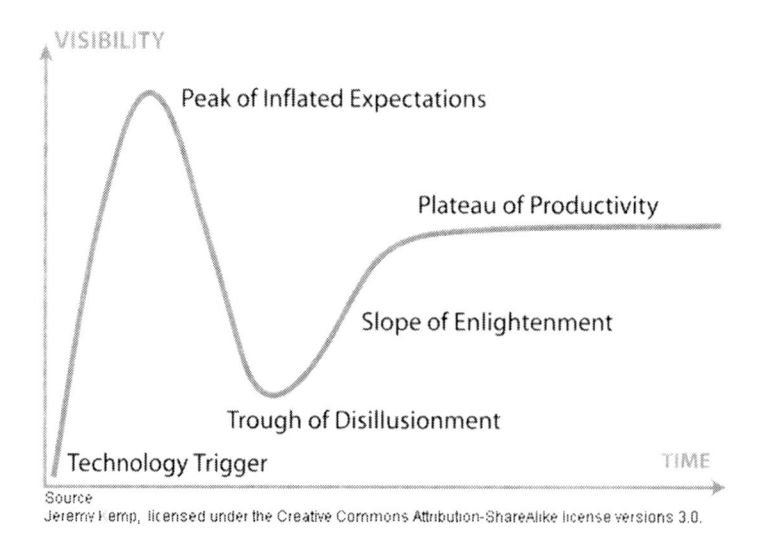

Figure 2.2

Technology Trigger

At some point, developments in technology make a certain application possible. For cloud computing, we can state that the technology trigger was the emergence of virtualization. Virtualization made it possible to abstract the platform away from the underlying hardware, and this is one of the key elements behind cloud computing.

The Peak of Inflated Expectations

Initially, every popular technology will pass through a phase where there are more people talking about it than there are users. Early adopters will be raving about the new technology, and the press will be all over it. Many people will start to have expectations that are unrealistic. The technology will be seen as a magic solution to all the world's problems. Gartner positioned cloud computing at this peak in 2009. There wasn't an IT magazine that didn't use the word "cloud" and pointy-haired bosses across the globe were impressing their golf buddies by explaining how they pushed "everything to the cloud."

Trough of Disillusionment

If expectations are inflated, there will come a time when those expectations are proven to be too high, and the technology gets some negative feedback. From what we see around us, cloud computing is currently (2011) moving through this trough of disillusionment. We hear people say things such as: "The cloud is over-hyped"; "It's just a marketing term"; "it's just a new word for things we've been doing all along". That last remark is one that is very familiar to most PHP developers, because we've seen something happen recently with another technology: Ajax. The technology trigger for that happened long before the term was coined; it became possible to call server side requests from the browser and process the results. Ajax was the next big thing, and was hyped and mocked by people for being just a new name for old technology, but it survived this Trough of Disillusionment and went on to build the next web on the Slope of Enlightenment.

Slope of Enlightenment

The Slope of Enlightenment is the next phase in a technology's life cycle, according to Gartner. This is when the hype has died down and people start to slowly realize how to make use of the technology effectively. The amount of vendors in the cloud space is increasing, offering tools to manage and build clouds, which indicates that a significant portion of the world has embraced cloud technology and is starting to use it effectively in real-life scenarios.

Plateau of Productivity

When a technology becomes mainstream, it has reached the Plateau of Productivity. One important thing to realize is that at this point, a technology has become a common resource in the developer's toolset. For example, with Ajax there is no longer much talk about the technology; it's simply become a standard skill for client-side-oriented PHP developers. This will happen to cloud computing as well. In a number of years, cloud computing will be a commodity and it will be a part of our daily work. When Gartner placed cloud computing in The Peak of Inflated Expectations in 2009, they also predicted that in two to three years cloud computing would be mainstream. At the time of writing, we are slowly getting there, and if you read this in 2011 or beyond it may be a reality. Regardless, even if you read this book before that happens, you are on the right track. If a technology becomes mainstream, you should be prepared to adopt it. And the early adopters will have the benefit of knowing everything about the cloud when the masses start using it.

Alright then, let's have a closer look at the three service models that are part of cloud computing.

Infrastructure as a Service

A web application cannot live without infrastructure. It is the foundation upon which the application is built. Infrastructure typically consists of a number of layers:

The Network is the connections between machines and the conduits that transport data through applications.

The Hardware includes the servers, processors and other physical items that make up the hardware on which applications run.

Whether you are running Linux, Solaris, Windows or a flavor of Unix, there's no application without an **Operating System** to provide core system functionality.

The **Storage** layer contains the hard disks that provide storage for the data that our applications process.

System Software is the glue between the application, the operating system and the data in the storage is formed by the system software running on the servers. This includes web server software such as Apache and database software such as MySQL or Oracle.

Traditionally, these five layers always had to be present to be able to run an application. Infrastructure as a Service is a paradigm in which these five layers are no longer required to be physically present but where they can be used as an on-demand service. Amazon, one of the leading companies in the Infrastructure as a Service space, provides services in most of the above five layers (we'll have a look at Amazon's services later in the book). They started out by offering the infrastructure they had in place for their own applications to interested parties. Amazon had a massive amount of servers to be able to handle the load a company like theirs attracts. However, their servers weren't always fully utilized and at some point they thought that companies might be interested in renting Amazon's infrastructure when it was not used by Amazon itself. This form of pooling resources between users is one of the important characteristics of cloud computing we saw earlier.

Infrastructure as a Service is typically provided as a set of APIs that offer access to infrastructure resources. The APIs allow you, for example, to create virtual machine instances, or to store or retrieve data from a storage or database.

The main benefit of virtualized infrastructure that is offered as a service is scalability. The commercial model is that you pay for the infrastructure that you actually use. This means that you don't have expensive servers idling, and if there is a spike in your visitor numbers, you don't have to worry if the hardware will cope. You simply scale the infrastructure up and down as needed. Since the servers are virtual, it's much easier to create a new one (as we'll see later in the book, it can be done with a few lines of PHP code), than it was to add a new box to a server farm.

Another advantage of Infrastructure as a Service is that you can stop worrying about the infrastructure. In the past, if a hard disk failed, most system administrators would have to take action immediately. Of course, virtual storage that is offered as a service still works with physical hard disks a few layers down, but the main difference is that those physical disks are no longer your problem. You purchase storage as a service from a vendor, and it's the vendor's responsibility to make sure it works. The layer of virtualization makes it easier to deal with hardware problems. Instead of worrying about the loss of data, a typical scenario is that a virtual machine is simply moved to a different physical box at the first sign of trouble.

Infrastructure as a Service is very similar to working with actual physical infrastructure, but it's generally easier. You pay only for what you actually use and you have to worry less about the intricacies of managing infrastructure; you can effectively make this someone else's problem. In that sense it's very similar to managed hosting. The difference, though, is that instead of calling your hosting provider to add a new physical box, you can do that through a self-service interface or you could even write a script that adds virtual boxes as needed.

Platform as a Service

With Infrastructure as a Service, every part of the infrastructure is abstracted and available to us as a service. With Platform as a Service, we move a step further. We no longer have to deal with every element of the infrastructure; instead, we can regard the system as one solid platform. This is best explained with an example. In the case of Infrastructure as a Service, if you have a website that suddenly requires more capacity because the amount of visitors increased, you would typically fire up more virtual machine instances. With Platform as a Service, this is no longer the case; the platform will scale up and down as necessary and takes care of the implementation details. The platform is typically represented to you as a single box. If you're old enough to remember turbo buttons on 386 computers back in the early nineties, then this is pretty much similar. If your app requires it, the turbo switches on and the platform offers more capacity. Your app doesn't notice it, it just has more capacity (cpu cycles, memory, storage, etc.) available.

Since the platform usually acts as if it were a single box, it's much easier to work with, and generally you don't have to change much in your application to be able to run on a Platform as a Service environment.

PaaS doesn't only offer cpu, memory or file storage; other parts of the infrastructure are often available as well, such as databases, either in the form of a scaling traditional RDBMS system, or one of the 'NoSQL' databases that are currently gaining momentum.

While for application developers a Platform as a Service environment is much easier, it's typically more difficult for the hosting providers. Infrastructure as a Service is already pretty much commoditized; there are virtualization products widely available to set up a hosting platform that can offer virtual machine images to clients. Platform as a Service, on the other hand, typically requires specific software setups in order to hide away all the infrastructure implementation details and provide a single platform to the end user. Perhaps this is why there aren't many Platform as a Service solutions for PHP available yet, as we'll notice in Chapter 6.

Software as a Service

The third available service model goes another step further in the realm of abstraction. We no longer care about infrastructure as with Infrastructure as a Service, nor do we care about the platform, as with Platform as a Service. This time, we only need to worry about the applications we're dealing with. Good examples of Software as a Service are the popular CRM application Salesforce or the online office applications offered by Google Apps. Where in the past you had to install software on the desktop, you can now use this software "as a service"; you just create an account and you are ready to use the apps, in the comfort of your web browser.

The Software as a Service model is one that, on the surface, is targeted more directly at end users than at developers. Software as a Service is more than just applications, as we'll see later on in this section, but let's start by looking at these end-user applications. If they are readily available to our users, then how can they be interesting for us developers? For developers it's interesting to see how we can create applications that can interact with existing Software as a Service applications or how we can interact with these applications to be able to customize them or integrate them. We'll look at this aspect of Software as a Service later in the book.

So when is software "Software as a Service"? Isn't any web application offered as a service? To some extent, yes; but with Software as a Service we are usually dealing with "multi tenant" applications, meaning there is one application that services multiple customers. The distinction is subtle, but it's easily explained with an example that every PHP developer is familiar with. We've all developed a Content Management System at some point in our career (I still have to meet the first PHP developer that never had to build or install a CMS system). The typical CMS is installed to service one customer. Multiple users generally, but one customer. If you have two customers, you'll typically have two installations of a CMS. The same CMS, two different versions of the same CMS, or two different CMS systems entirely. Moving your CMS to a "Software as a Service" model would mean that there are no longer multiple, different instances of your CMS; you'd have one environment that services all your customers. This "multi-tenancy" has implications for the way we deploy applications, so we'll look closer at multi tenant architecture in the Architecture chapter later on.

For developers the most interesting aspect of Software as a Service is that it's not limited to end-user applications. There is an enormous amount of services that application developers can use as components when developing applications. An example of this is Payment services. Instead of having to write your own credit/debit card payment interfaces, and instead of installing software libraries that implement these services, you can use online payment providers that offer their solution as a service; these can be integrated seamlessly in your application. This form of software as a service is very popular, and the amount of services available for integration is enormous. We'll look at some of the available services in Chapter 7.

Software as a Service (both the end-user applications and the reusable-component services) is true to the cloud characteristic of "metered use." Typically users pay monthly fees to be able to use a piece of software as opposed to the traditional license and upgrade fees. Developers integrating components typically pay fees based on the usage of the components; some services offer 'per request' fees where you pay based on the amount of requests you send to a service; others offer monthly fees where rates depend on the service level you require (with support, without support, etc.)

Chapter 3

Cloud Basics

In this chapter, we'll give you a heads-up on some of the basic techniques you have to grasp before you dive into cloud computing. We'll explain the concepts and why it's important to be familiar with them. We won't be able to teach you all of the details of the topics in this chapter; whole books have been written about each of these topics. But we'll cover enough information to give you a basic understanding, sufficient to let you work with the code exercises we will go through in this book. Let's look at the prerequisites for working with cloud services in PHP. We'll be brief with the prerequisites because we want to get to the cool parts of cloud computing soon. Feel free to glance through this chapter and skip whatever you already understand.

General Prerequisites

PHP

It's fairly obvious that you should be comfortable with PHP itself, but we want to mention it anyway. If you are new to PHP or this is the first book you read, you may want to put the book aside for a little while and have a look at php|architect's PHP Essentials training courses. Yes, that was a shameless plug for one of our publisher's additional services, but the take-away here is that this book is written for people who are already comfortable with PHP.

Object-Oriented Development

Many cloud services work with object-oriented concepts. If services offer a PHP library to make it easier to work with the services from PHP, then these libraries are often written in object-oriented fashion. This is not only because OO is the most popular programming paradigm; it's probably also because cloud services are generally language agnostic, and many modern languages are OO. Unlike PHP, many languages do not offer a hybrid OO/Procedural approach; Java and Ruby, for example, are OO languages and do not offer procedural programming. To keep cloud libraries and services consistent, you'll therefore see that most of the PHP implementations are written in OO PHP as well.

This means that you'll work a lot with OO. If your work in PHP has mostly involved procedural programming, you will want to take a crash course in OO. There are many books on OO development; if you'll allow us to plug another one of php|architect's courses, then their Professional PHP course is the one to attend.

OO isn't very difficult; in fact, the entire universe is "object oriented". OO is all about objects and the actions we can perform on them. Your procedural update_page() PHP function will become page->update(). The page is an object and "update" is one of the actions we can perform on it. Simple, huh? OK, there's a lot more to OO than this one-line primer, but this book is not about OO. Just make sure you're comfortable with OO concepts before you start dealing with clouds.

Network Programming

Clouds are generally highly connected. Virtual machine instances communicate among each other to exchange and synchronize data. Platform as a Service components are integrated through the use of APIs; this means that when dealing with clouds, we will get to do a lot of network programming. Luckily PHP offers high-level functions for dealing with the network. It's generally not necessary to do socket-level network connections where we need to define our own protocols. Most communication within the cloud is based on the familiar HTTP protocol, which we already know from our everyday web development.

One of the most common ways to deal with network programming in PHP is through the use of the cURL extension. We'll be using cURL quite a bit throughout the book, so let's start with some simple examples to get familiarized with the extension. Essentially, cURL is like a built-in browser within PHP. Not that it will render webpages, but it can connect to URLs, retrieve their content and post data to the network. Below is a code snippet that shows you the basic usage of cURL.

```
$ch = curl_init();

curl_setopt($ch, CURLOPT_URL, "http://api.cloudphp.net/");
curl_setopt($ch, CURLOPT_HEADER, false);
curl_setopt($ch, CURLOPT_RETURNTRANSFER, true);

$content = curl_exec($ch);

curl_close($ch);
```

On the first line, we initialize cURL and retrieve a handle we can work with. What might seem confusing is the way we control cURL; we use curl_setopt to tell cURL what to do. In this case, we're setting three options. The first option tells cURL that we want to retrieve the http://api.cloudphp.net URL. The second option tells cURL that for now we're not interested in the HTTP header. If we leave out this option then the HTTP header fields are included in the output. Since generally we're more interested in the content, you'll see that in most cases you will want to set this to false. (We'll show a more convenient way to retrieve the header in a minute). The third option tells cURL that we want the content that was retrieved to be returned in a variable. If we don't specify this option, cURL will send its output straight to the end user's browser. Since we'll be using cURL mostly to talk to APIs and we don't want to burden our end users with the output from them, CURLOPT_RETURNTRANSFER' is an essential option.

The next line tells cURL to do its work, retrieve the output and store it in the $content variable. Finally we do a bit of cleanup and tell cURL that we're done and no longer need the cURL handle.

By default, cURL will send a GET request to the URL we are retrieving. In some cases you will want to send a POST request and send post data to an API. In that case, you can use these options:

```
$data = array('someparam' => 'somevalue');
curl_setopt($ch, CURLOPT_POSTFIELDS, $data);
curl_setopt($ch, CURLOPT_POST, true);
```

22 ■ Cloud Basics

These options tell cURL to execute a POST request and send $data as variables along with the request.

When working with APIs, you may also be interested in the header that a URL sends to you. We used an option to make sure the header is not part of the retrieved content, because that would mean that we'd have to parse the header from the content ourselves. It's much easier to use the function `curl_getinfo` to retrieve information about the request:

```
$info = curl_getinfo($ch);
$httpstatus = $info['http_code']; // 200 for OK, 404 not found etc
```

The `curl_getinfo` function retrieves some other useful metadata, such as how long the request takes; this is useful when hunting performance bottlenecks.

We've looked at the common use cases for cURL, but cURL can do a lot more than the above examples. If you want to learn more about this extension, visit the cURL page[1] in the PHP documentation to read about the details.

XML

Many APIs send their results as XML data. This is very useful, since it's human readable, so easy to debug, and there are a few different PHP options for working with XML. For most APIs, you'll find that the easy-to-use SimpleXML functions in PHP are sufficient. Consider the following XML message:

```
<?xml version="1.0" encoding="UTF-8"?>
<books>
  <book title="PHP in the Cloud" pages="100" />
</books>
```

SimpleXML makes it very easy to parse this. Let's suppose that the $content variable from the cURL example above contains this XML message. We can then retrieve the book title and the page count using the following code snippet:

```
$xml = simplexml_load_string($content);
```

---

[1] http://www.php.net/curl

```
$title = $xml->book["title"];
$pages = $xml->book["pages"];
```

The variable $xml is an object created by simplexml_load_string. We don't have to worry about the <books></books> tags because $xml itself is an object representation of this root element. We can then easily retrieve a child object ('book') in this case using object-oriented syntax. Attributes (the title="") from the example are available as array elements within the book object.

This shows how easy it is to work with XML documents, which makes PHP an excellent language to deal with APIs. There is more information on SimpleXML[2] in the PHP documentation.

You may run into occasions where SimpleXML doesn't cut it. It's called SimpleXML because it's built to deal with simple XML use cases. In the situations where it doesn't work or is not sufficient, you can use the DOM extension[3]. It's slightly more complicated but much more powerful. In reality, we've found that API providers will want as many people as possible to be able to use their APIs, so generally their XML formats aren't overly complex. This means that probably over 80% of the use cases can be handled using SimpleXML, so use that as your starting point when dealing with XML in the cloud.

JSON

JSON is, like XML, a data-exchange format. It has become very popular as an interchange format because it's more compact than XML, but still quite human readable.

JSON is a JavaScript representation of a piece of data, hence the name JavaScript Object Notation. The fact that it's JavaScript is another reason it's very popular; it can be directly interpreted by the JavaScript engine in web browsers, making this a popular data format for Ajax requests.

Here's the book example from the previous section as a JSON message (Note that the newlines have been added for readability. It's known that json_decode will choke on newlines so place everything on one line if you want to parse this message.):

```
{
```

---

[2] http://www.php.net/simplexml
[3] http://www.php.net/dom

```
    "book":{
       "title":"PHP in the Cloud",
       "pages":"100"
    }
}
```

If `$content` contains such a JSON payload, then we can easily parse this message with the code shown below:

```
$json = json_decode($jcontent);
echo $json->book->title;
echo $json->book->pages;
```

It doesn't get any easier than this. To encode data as JSON you'd call `json_encode`. The JSON extension is enabled by default in PHP. More information can be found on the JSON page[4] in the PHP documentation.

Virtualization

The next topic we want to familiarize you with is Virtualization. It's not that hard, fortunately. Imagine a server. Imagine the big metal box with the CPU, the hard drives, a set of cables. Imagine connecting to the server using an SSH session, typing "`ls`" (or "`dir`" if you're a Windows person), hearing its hard drives spin up and seeing the results of the directory listing appear on screen. This is familiar, right?

Now imagine having that same server in a hosting facility, somewhere across the country. You log in through SSH, type "`ls`" or "`dir`", but you no longer hear the hard drive spin up because the server is far away. You still get the results as before, just without the sound of physical hard-drive activity. If you wished, you could go to the hosting facility, find your server and listen to the soothing sounds of the hard drive spinning.

Now, finally, imagine going to that hosting facility and discovering that your server is not there. You can SSH into the box and work with it, but a server is nowhere to be found. You panic and ask the guy at the reception where your server is. The guy laughs at you, telling you that your server is virtual. It exists in cyberspace, on a

---
[4] http://www.php.net/json

central big hardware platform along with its other server friends, but it no longer has a physical manifestation in your server room. There, that's virtualization. Stuff you can work with without it being there. You'll have to find something else to sooth you if you miss the hard-drive spinning sounds, but once you're used to the idea of not having that physical box you can touch, you'll find that you can still work with it as if it is a physical server. This is your first step toward enlightenment: when you start understanding that once your server is no longer physically there, it's much easier to own 10 servers or hundreds of servers, all virtual and not taking up any space.

One way to familiarize yourself with virtual servers is to install the free VMWare Player[5], download a couple of so-called appliances[6] and play around with them. The first time you fire up a virtual server right there on your own workstation you will feel like you've created life with your bare hands!

Another way to work with virtual servers that do not run on your own workstation is to rent yourself a VPS. Slicehost[7] is one of the many developer-friendly Virtual Private Server providers that offers Virtual Servers from USD 20 per month.

Virtualization of servers (virtual machines) is one of the most common virtualization techniques, but essentially anything can be virtualized, from the network to storage. In those cases it's again a matter of leaving the physical world behind and learning to deal with the fact that you can work with hardware even though you can't touch it; it exists only in the realm of the digital. (Of course, under the hood everything still runs on hardware, but you can consider that hardware "out of your reach"; it's the hardware infrastructure that the virtual world resides on but that we no longer have dealings with.)

Clustering

If machines become virtual, it is easier to have many of them. If you have many, then you need to have a way to piece them together into an architecture. The technique to combine multiple machines is generally called clustering.

---

[5] http://www.vmware.com/products/player/
[6] http://www.vmware.com/appliances/
[7] http://www.slicehost.com/

Luckily, the fact that we're being virtual in clouds makes clustering easy. Loadbalancing, redundancy and other features typically associated with server clusters are generally taken care of by the cloud providers.

One important thing to learn about clustering is that it's not a silver bullet to make an application instantly scale. An application that is not equipped to run on multiple servers simultaneously will break if we scale it across multiple virtual instances. Especially if the application has bottlenecks such as resources that only one server may use at a time (such as some very traditional database setups), you'll need to adapt the application to be able to run on multiple servers.

For now there's not much to tell. We'll look at bottleneck prevention in more detail in the next chapter, which deals with architecture.

Web Services

We've already covered network programming, XML and Rest in the general prerequisites. The more general topic that we should discuss now is web services. Web services are basically services provided using web technologies; they are essentially the APIs that allow applications to interact with each other. There are three basic web service protocols that we'll briefly discuss; they are the most common in use on the Web right now and we'll work with these three throughout the book when we talk about cloud services.

SOAP

SOAP is short for Simple Object Access Protocol. It is a protocol that was intended to have applications interact with each other in a sort of object-oriented fashion, regardless of the technology used on either side. If someone had a Java object that could perform certain actions, then someone using a completely different language could call the methods on that Java object remotely. To do this, SOAP consists of a protocol that wraps messages sent to objects in a so-called envelope (essentially an XML message with a payload), and relies on translations from a technology- specific object to a language-independent-object notation. Then on the other site the protocol compiles that notation back into a call to an object.

To effectively do this mapping, SOAP preferably uses a so-called WSDL file (pronounced as 'wiz-del') - short for Web Service Description Language. This is a file that describes the available objects, the types of the data it understands and the methods that are callable.

SOAP is considered a 'heavy' protocol because it has some overhead and working with WSDL's can be quite cumbersome. Nevertheless, SOAP is very easy to work with from PHP. The code below shows a code snippet calling a SOAP service from PHP using PHP's built-in SOAP extension:

```
$helloObj = new SoapClient( "http://api.cloudphp.net/Hello.wsdl");

$helloObj->sayHello("world");
```

In this example, we see the ease of use PHP provides. The SoapClient class takes a WSDL file and then creates an actual PHP object that represents the remote class. We can then call the sayHello method on this class and give it some parameters. Under the hood, this call is translated and sent over the network to the object actually implementing the sayHello call (which could be a PHP object, a Java object, a .NET object, you name it).

If you want to learn more about SOAP, you could look at the documentation for PHP's SOAP extension[8]. It is, however, quite lacking; it doesn't even explain the simple concept of creating an object. (Instead you'll find documentation on its internal methods that are internal to the object and that you generally never call). It's better to do a search on the Web for 'php soapclient tutorial' that will help you find numerous posts explaining how it works. But the above code snippet pretty much describes the essentials.

REST

The REST protocol is more popular than SOAP, because it's more lightweight and doesn't require WSDL files, translations or envelopes. REST basically uses the concepts that are already available to us in the HTTP specification to create a protocol for interaction between applications.

---

[8] http://www.php.net/soap

REST, which is short for REpresentational State Transfer. It's not a great acronym because even when you hear 'representational state transfer' it still doesn't convey much. REST deals with resources, and resources can be anything (a book, a user, a product in an e-shop) and they are represented by a URL. The following URL can be considered a resource representing a user: `http://cloudphp.net/user/joe`.

REST then uses the HTTP methods POST, GET, PUT and DELETE to manipulate this resource. Sending an HTTP POST request to this URL with certain values in the post fields, will update the user with the new data. POST updates an object, GET retrieves an object, PUT creates an object and DELETE deletes it.

The output of such a request can by anything, but generally XML and JSON are acceptable output formats for REST requests. The output of a POST request on the above user URL could be an XML message containing the updated details for user Joe.

Because REST uses conventional HTTP mechanisms, you will not find REST functions in PHP, unlike SOAP, which has its own built-in extension. Instead, you will normally use something like cURL to pass requests to REST services. The Wikipedia page for REST[9] has more information if you would like to get into details.

HTTP APIs

Pure REST APIs use the four mentioned HTTP verbs, nothing more. REST fans will tell you that any action can be modeled after the HTTP protocol with just these four verbs. Consider the action "calculate basket". This would basically be a POST request to a basket resource. "Add item to shopping cart" would be that same POST request, but with a new item passed along in the POST fields.

Trying to get your head around this can be difficult, however, which is why many web services have resorted to a slightly less "RESTful" REST implementation. Instead of pure resource URLS, they accept arbitrary URLs that contain not only a resource but also actions: `http://api.cloudphp.net/basket/additem?item_id=3` `http://api.cloudphp.net/user/joe?action=unregister`

Aside from being a little less strict on the "Every URL must be a resource! Every action must be an HTTP verb!" adage, working with HTTP APIs is similar to working

---
[9] `http://en.wikipedia.org/wiki/Representational_State_Transfer`

with REST, although you'll find that most HTTP APIs usually only use GET and POST, not PUT and DELETE.

'HTTP API' is not a formal name, nor is it a formal protocol; it's generally used to implicate any web service that works via the HTTP protocol but that does not follow the REST principles.

System Administration

The final basic skill you will need in order to work efficiently with clouds is system administration. Even if you're a developer, there are a few basic things you've got to learn how to do, such as logging in to a server through SSH and entering some commands, or logging in to a Windows management interface and configuring a web server.

Windows management is not so hard for PHP developers. If you are familiar with how Windows works then you'll pretty much point and click your way through most configuration challenges, helped by a web search engine to look up the options that sound unfamiliar.

Linux, on the other hand, can be a bit harder; the commandline can be scary if you've never used one. But when you are dealing with Infrastructure as a Service, you may have to deal with the virtual infrastructure using command-line tools, so it might be a good idea to dive into Linux command-line usage. We won't have the opportunity to give you a crash course in Linux, but our friend Lorna Mitchell has a great 'Linux-Fu' presentation that she regularly presents at conferences. It is specifically targeted at PHP developers, and the slides[10] are available online. This will help you learn the basic commands, and can be helpful to look up what a command does when you see us using one in the book.

---

[10] http://www.slideshare.net/lornajane/linuxfu-for-php-developers

Chapter 4

Cloud Architecture

Now that we've covered some of the basic skills that are useful when working with clouds, we're going to cover some more advanced things, by looking at some of the architectural topics that are relevant when developing for "the Cloud". Building applications while keeping in mind the architectural recommendations from this chapter will make your applications more "cloud friendly".

Horizontal Scalability

Horizontal scalability is the ability of a computing entity to increase its computing power and memory by incorporating additional servers. This is different from vertical scalability, which depends on the addition of resources to an existing server. Horizontal scalability is not a given when running an application on a cloud environment; it's something we often have to build into our applications. Considering that PaaS and SaaS clouds abstract the infrastructure away, it's logical that these clouds automatically scale horizontally, but IaaS clouds usually leave the details of implementing horizontal scalability to the developers.

Traditionally, horizontal scalability is achieved by clustering. Let's look at a few typical infrastructure setups that provide us with horizontal scalability. Figure 4.1 is an example of a horizontally scalable architecture.

This picture could depict a physical system setup, but in an IaaS cloud, the setup from Figure 4.1 can be built with virtual machine instances.

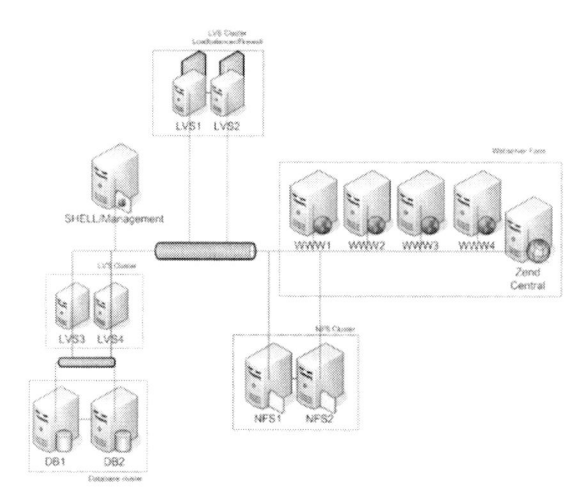

Figure 4.1

Another potential architecture for horizontal scalability is a PaaS cloud. One of the defining benefits of a PaaS cloud is that it abstracts the need to manage individual server instances, so in this case the architecture looks more like Figure 4.2.

We can also build an architecture that partially relies on SaaS cloud services to reap the benefit of automatic horizontal scaling inherent in those services. We could, for example, start out with an IaaS cloud, but instead of managing our own database, we could decide to use a Software as a Service component for data storage. Figure 4.3 displays an example of such a hybrid IaaS-with-SaaS components approach.

There is no "One Architecture To Rule Them All"; evaluate your options carefully and build a scalable architecture that meets your needs. You can, however, use the following guidelines when choosing your architecture.

The IaaS architecture depicted in Figure 4.1 is useful if you need fine-grained control over the application environment, configuration and versions.

The PaaS architecture from Figure 4.2 is ideal when you are building a new application from scratch and do not want to worry about scaling now or in the future. If you don't foresee any special fine-grained control requirements then a worry-free PaaS environment is a suitable architecture.

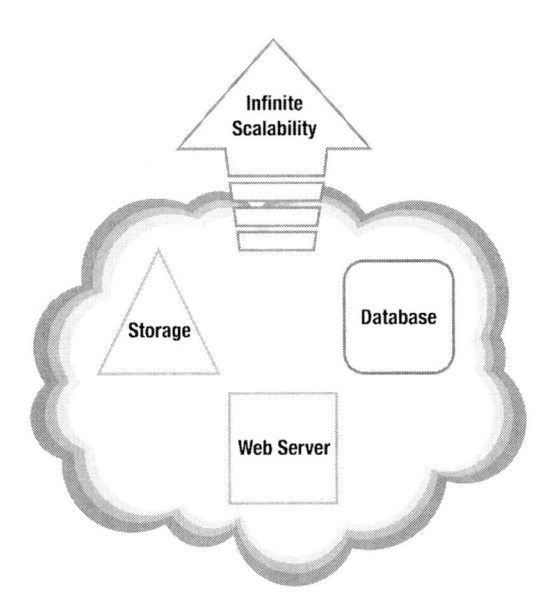

Figure 4.2

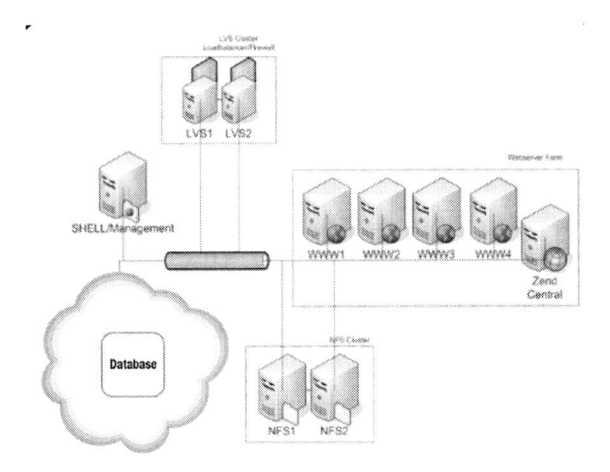

Figure 4.3

The IaaS/Saas hybrid model from Figure 4.3 may be the way to go if you are looking to take a piece-meal approach to migrate an application to the cloud or when you are unable to do a full PaaS migration due to special requirements at certain parts of the infrastructure.

Other considerations when choosing an overall architecture for a cloud are cost considerations, support and maintenance requirements and, of course, the familiarity of your team with any of these approaches.

While SaaS and PaaS clouds manage all the details of horizontal scaling, in the case of IaaS this burden is on the developer. What does it take to create a horizontally scalable application on an IaaS cloud? Would your existing applications be able to live within a horizontally scalable architecture? Let's take a look at some of the techniques and tools in the implementation of a horizontally scalable architecture.

Load-balancing

There are different areas to consider when load-balancing, but all considerations begin with setting your performance and quality of service expectations. Usually, the potential to be infinitely scalable via incrementing resources requires major changes to the logical architecture, to make sure that components continue to work in an optimal way in the scaled environment.

Once you have the right expectations in place, you'll need to identify parts of your overall architecture where load-balancing is necessary to achieve the expected level of performance. First, take a look at your application's clients and services. "Clients" refers to any possible consumers that logical groupings of servers within your architecture may have. These can be internal, e.g., a group of database servers serving web servers; or external, e.g., web servers which in turn serve browser requests. "Services", on the other hand, refers to the services that the logical grouping of servers provide. The logical grouping of web servers, for example, responds to requests for service originating via the HTTP protocol. In Figure 4.1 that we showed earlier you can see a few of these groups: there's a web group, a database group and a storage group.

The key is to make sure that logical groupings of servers are able to provide services to their clients optimally. For example, a website that serves most of its contents via a cache on the web server will require high scalability on the end of the web servers and less on the database end. A transaction-heavy application that interacts a lot with the database will need high scalability on the database end.

By grouping things into logical sections, we are able to find out where scalability is required by looking at services and clients. Scalability for machines can typically be achieved by what is called 'Layer 4' load-balancing. (The layer numbers refer to the layers from the OSI network model which you may remember from computer science class. If not, don't worry, it's not important; the name doesn't really matter in our case.) Layer 4 load balancing, also known as "transport layer load-balancing", involves distributing TCP and UDP (and some other less popular protocol) connections and requests from the load-balancer server to several other servers that actually manage the request. Several distribution algorithms exist, such as "round-robin", "least-connection" and "shortest expected delay".

Since we cannot install hardware in the cloud, we'll have to rely on software load-balancers instead, which we install on a server instance within the IaaS cloud. IPVS is an open-source software load-balancer for those looking for a free solution that they can control. It is one of the oldest software-based load-balancers available and supports routing via NAT (Network Address Translation; changing the destination address of a packet), IP tunneling (wrapping the IP datagram within another datagram) and direct routing by rewriting the MAC address.

Layer 4 load balancing is smart, but in a limited way. It only knows to reroute packets to a certain number of machines, regardless of the purpose of these machines. To make the load-balancing a bit smarter we can use "layer 7" load balancing. Layer-7 load-balancing involves parsing the request at the application layer to find out the requested content and route the request to a server that can host the content optimally. This way, we are able to create content servers that are specialized hosts of specific contents. For example, we could route video streaming to a group of servers that has a large storage capacity and route caching requests to servers with larger amounts of memory.

There are many ways to perform layer-7 load-balancing with supporting open-source software such as KTCPVS and HAProxy. There are also modules for web servers such as Apache, Lighttpd and nginx, and HTTP accelerators such as Varnish that enables load-balancing as a reverse proxy. Commercially, Zeus Load Balancer is a very comprehensive product that supports both layer 4 and layer 7 load-balancing.

It is conveniently available in several versions: as software, as a Virtual Appliance or as an Amazon Machine Image (AMI) on Amazon EC2.

We won't go into the details of these products as this would make the book more suitable for system administrators. All the mentioned products are very easy to look up though, if you want to play around with them.

Parallel Distributed Job Processing

Horizontal scalability can be even more fine-grained when we're not just routing requests to servers, but routing specific workloads with job distribution frameworks such as Gearman[1] and other message queues. We will build an example with distributed job processing in Chapter 5.

Sessions

PHP sessions are used extensively in many web applications as a way to maintain state, since HTTP in itself is a stateless protocol. By default sessions are stored on the local server on which the PHP requests are executed. This however will cause a problem when we scale horizontally by load-balancing: requests may be routed to a server that did not create the initial session, and thus have no record of the session at all. A typical symptom of this is that your users start noticing unintended logouts, or loss of their shopping carts, as soon as you start load balancing your application across multiple machines. To solve this problem, we will need to ensure that our sessions are horizontally scalable.

There are several ways to tackle the problem. An easy solution is making sure that requests from the same client always go to the same server. Another solution is implementing some form of shared session storage, and the third is session clustering. The first solution can be implemented by using load-balancers that support "session affinity", but this is rather cumbersome in many ways. For one, it could lead to one server being hogged by a heavy user while other servers are still idle. The second solution involves storing sessions into databases or within a shared file storage, but there are obviously communication and other overheads that may affect performance.

---

[1] http://pecl.php.net/package/gearman/

Session clustering, on the other hand, is an increasingly popular way to manage sessions in a horizontally scalable environment. It involves the synchronization of session data across servers within a cluster, with managed failure recovery. It is a feature available within Zend Platform, a specialized commercial PHP web-application server. It is also possible to implement a form of session clustering using the distributed-memory caching solution "memcached". In this case you'll need to implement a good structure that manages server cluster information so the apps know where to find the sessions in memcached.

Distributed File-storage

Another feature that may prevent applications from scaling horizontally is file storage. In most PHP applications when files are uploaded or created on the spot, they are stored on a directory on the web server. If we move to a multi-server environment, this may cause trouble; if a user uploads his avatar picture while on server 1, and another user later views his profile while on server 2, the image is not there. The traditional approach to solve this problem was to add a shared storage, i.e. disk space that was used by all the web servers. While this is a good solution in some scenarios, it's not exactly horizontally scalable. If the number of web servers grows, the shared storage gets more and more load.

A solution that is more horizontally scalable than shared storage is to use cloud-based storage offerings such as Amazon S3 and Rackspace Cloudfiles. A disadvantage of such services, however, can be the speed of file transfer over the Internet, since you'll be constantly transferring files from your web-server instances to these cloud providers. This can be overcome if you host other parts of your application within the same provider network (e.g., hosting an application on Amazon's EC2 while storing your files on Amazon S3), but there's another possibility: building your very own distributed file-storage within your infrastructure. This could be a viable and more cost-efficient option, depending on your setup.

A distributed file storage within your existing infrastructure could be as simple as reservering some disk space on all your web server instances and using that for distributed storage. Of course, you'll need a management layer to keep track of where the files are and to retrieve them from the right instance, and there are a few prominent open-source distributed file-storage solutions available that can do this for you. Three of the most commonly used, distributed file-storage solutions are MogileFS2[2], HDFS3 (Hadoop Distributed File System[3] and Ceph[4]. For a typical PHP environment, MogileFS is highly practical and flexible. It can be installed rather unobtrusively on plain hardware and works by running 'mogilefsd' daemons, generally referred to as "trackers", to manage the various communications involved in a file-storage system. Trackers listen to an application when it requests placement of a file on a storage node. It handles replication, as well as all metadata required to keep the file-storage working. The metadata is stored in a database. It is important that the database used to store the metadata is fault tolerant, as the file-storage relies on it heavily. A PECL extension is available to aide an application's communication with MogileFS trackers[5].

Besides supporting horizontal scalability, a distributed file-storage provides other forms of benefits, such as automatic replication to enhance fault tolerance, so it's definitely worth having a look at.

Automatic Deployment

Applications that scale to multiple machine instances require some thinking about the way these machines are configured and about how applications are deployed on them. In a typical growth scenario you may set up the first instance manually, and for the second instance you will be looking closely at instance one and replicating what's on that instance. By the time you work with three server instances you will start thinking it's a brilliant idea to document the deployment process so that every server can easily be set up exactly the same way. Instance 4 is set up nicely according to the deployment documentation, but by the time you're firing up instance 8 you will almost have died of boredom, and when adding instance 9 you forget a crucial step because it has become routine, and routine jobs lead to mistakes. To prevent you from making this mistake, we're going to make you think about automatic deployment right from the start. And there's another good reason to do so: adding instances manually is very 2006; as we'll see elsewhere in this book you may be working with systems that add and remove instances as capacity requirements increase or

---

[2] http://www.danga.com/mogilefs/
[3] http://hadoop.apache.org/hdfs/
[4] http://ceph.newdream.net/
[5] http://pecl.php.net/package/mogilefs

decrease. With a system adding its own servers, you're going to have to automate the deployment of these servers, because you don't want to be connected to your cloud in a way that allows it to use the words, "Dave, I've added 15 new server instances to the primary core. Please install." So let's look at ways to automate deployment.

Server instances are usually spawned from a single image and have exactly the same environment setup. There are many ways to deploy new releases on these instances. We may, for example, set up a cron job on the master image to check for new releases at a pre-determined interval and update itself with the new releases. Servers instantiated from this master image will then inherit this trait and do the same. This setup has to be done really carefully though, and is only suitable for certain environments where the application and environment are tightly managed. We could also maintain a list of all spawned servers, and deliver the new release to these servers from some kind of deployment agent/script or use a tool such as Puppet[6] to help ensure consistency across all instances. Whatever it is, we want to avoid having to perform a lot of manual operations on each instance.

One quick and convenient option to deploy to multiple servers in a tightly managed environment is via the operating system's package management system (e.g. RPM[7], DEB[8]. A packaging system provides a uniformed way to deploy an application with the added benefit of having a standard upgrade path and rollback mechanism. On top of that, if the release involves any new extensions and related libraries, these dependencies can be specified and managed by the packaging system as well. Once set up, a package can be placed on a package repository where all server instances can update themselves with the latest release.

Let's explore the use of the Debian packaging system, since it is one of the most popular packaging systems around. There are two sides to this story: compiling your application into a package and installing these packages onto your instances. Mind you, we won't be teaching you all the ins and outs of the package system, just enough for practical application in your cloud environment.

---

[6] http://www.puppetlabs.com/puppet/
[7] http://rpm.org/
[8] http://www.debian.org/doc/FAQ/ch-pkgtools.en.html

Creating a Package for the Package Manager

To start packaging an application, create a directory called debian somewhere in your workspace. This debian directory will reflect the root of the system you are going to install your package on later. This means that if you put something in this debian/var/www directory, it will end up in /var/www/ on your machine once you install the package.

Place all your source files inside this debian directory, mimicking the layout of the system as you want it to be installed. Here's an example:

```
~/debian/var/www/mycoolapp/index.php
```

In this code, mycoolapp is the name of our application (and thus the name of our package).

To communicate some meta data about our application to the package system we need a bit more than just our sources. Inside the debian directory, you need to create a DEBIAN directory (mind the capitals) and place a file named 'control' with the following contents in it:

```
package: mycoolapp
Version: 1.0
Section: base
Priority: optional
Architecture: all
Maintainer: Vito Chin <vito@php.net>
Description: This is My Cool Application
```

You can leave section, priority and architecture to these defaults; the rest would be adjusted to your particular case.

Creating a package is then a simple matter of running the following command:

```
dpkg-deb --build debian mycoolapp.deb
```

We are assuming here that your PHP applications are deployed as source, but we are using a generic method of creating a binary debian package that can package just about anything. There are many other ways of creating a debian source or binary package that entail other steps that deal with specific needs, such as compilation specificity, documentation, etc., but we'll stick to the basics for now.

It can be tedious to have to build packages manually with every new release of your application. So we will provide you with an example of a script that can be used to ease the creation of the package:

```bash
#!/bin/bash
# deploy_app.sh

# Usage example: deploy_app.sh mycoolapp 1.0.2
# Assumes the application to be packaged is within the
# "debian" directory
# Update the DEBIAN/control file with the latest version information
find ./debian/DEBIAN/ -name 'control'
   -exec
      sed -i.bak 's/Version: .*/Version: '$2'/g' {} \;
# The above line assumes a current version of your app at the
# current location. You might replace this with an SVN checkout
# for example.

# Create the package.
dpkg-deb --build debian $1-$2.deb

# And then upload the package to our own package repository
scp $1-$2.deb vito@http://cloudphp.net:/var/www/repository/packages
# Clean up
rm *deb
```

When you run this script, specifying the package name and version number, it will create a package for it and upload it to a repository (we'll show how to create that repository in a minute).

You'll have to adjust this script to your needs; it's provided as an example. Don't blatantly copy and paste and run this, because the rm commands may be harmful if you're unsure whether the script uses the correct paths.

We used a bash script to automate part of this deployment process (the above is available within the accompanying source as deploy_app.sh), but any form of script (e.g. PHP) that can run on the console or other tools will do as well. Make sure the script (or any script you customize) is executable before running it:

```
chmod +x deploy_app.sh
```

Note that we have covered only actually installing the application into its document root. Another common consideration with PHP applications is changes within the database schema. While these deltas can be managed within a package as well (you can execute scripts whenever the package is installed on a server, and one of those could patch your database), developers should really consider the use of a cloud database if such IaaS-level automated elasticity is set up. It will be a complex endeavor managing a database on every instance of an automatically started server.

When you're moving into deployment automation, you should make sure that the deployment scripts are not accessible to the public, as they might be damaging if used in the wrong way. Especially if your deployment scripts are written in PHP, make sure they are not part of your regular publicly accessible document root; instead, keep them in a separate location only accessible by the system itself.

Creating a Repository

In one of the last steps of the script that we just created, the release package was uploaded to a package repository. This is useful because server instances can use this repository to check for new releases and upgrade themselves accordingly. Ideally, this repository should be private and hosted on a server within your cloud environment. A simple private repository can be quickly created by setting up an HTTP- or FTP-accessible directory with web-server based authentication.

In our example, we've assumed that your repository is located at `http://cloudphp.net/packages`, hosted from the document root `/var/www/repository/packages`. Creating this repository is simple. Create a directory named `binary` within the `packages` subdir and place all your `.deb` files into this directory. (In PHP, we generally don't deal with binaries, but the packaging system doesn't know that since it's a generic system for package management. Don't worry about this detail too much, just use `binaries` for the directory name as in our example.) Then from the packages directory, run:

```
dpkg-scanpackages binary | gzip -9c > binary/Packages.gz
```

This creates the metadata that turns our packages/binary directory into a Debian repository that can be used to install packages from. Assuming your web server is configured to serve the files (see if you can download the file `http://yoursevername/packages/mycoolapp-1.0.deb` from a browser), you now have a repository up and running. Now let's look at how to use this repository to deploy applications onto our web server instances.

Installing an Application From a Package on a Cloud Instance

Installing a package using Debian's package management system is fairly simple. It's generally a matter of executing the following command:

```
/usr/bin/apt-get install mycoolapp
```

By default, apt-get will not know your application; it wouldn't know where to get mycoolapp from. To make this work, we have to add the repository where we keep the mycoolapp packages to the sources for apt-get. Edit `/etc/apt/sources.list` and add the following line:

```
deb http://cloudphp.net/packages binary
```

You should use the repository URL we created in the previous section.

Note: you will want to perform these instructions on the virtual machine that acts as the master image from which all future instances will be created. This way, you set up the deployment only once, and every new image will use the same deployment mechanism.

To make all machines install new versions of the application automatically, we are going to automate the package-updating process on the master image. There are tools available to help with apt scheduling (e.g. cron-apt), but for a minimal case, some crontab entries will do. For example, if we want the server instance to check for new updates every hour, we could add the following lines to crontab:

```
* 01 * * * /usr/bin/apt-get install -y --force-yes mycoolapp
```

The apt-get install command will upgrade the package to the latest available version if it is already installed. The -y forces a 'yes' to any queries that might arise and -force=yes even assumes yes when apt-get is about to do something destructive, but we are automating deployment so we don't have the luxury to answer these questions manually. To counter the risks of using these options, we have to be confident that packages are safe and trustworthy, so implement good QA practices when you create new packages. Regression testing must be performed on the application by deploying it on a test server that mimics the environment of the live server instances with any new package dependencies in place. Packages should only be placed on the repository after it passes regression testing. This helps avoid possible problems caused somewhere within the dependency hierarchy, which may be very tedious to resolve, especially on an automatically elastic ecosystem of an IaaS-based cloud. Unit Tests are a strong recommendation as well. If your app is going to be automatically deployed after release, you must be very sure that it's stable.

Also, you might want to keep a close eye on the update process and check the logs regularly. However you'll notice that when you use a master image and all manual labor is replaced by scripts, that even though you may have many instances, they all behave in exactly the same way. So in that case your deployment process overall becomes more predictable.

Bottleneck Prevention

Bottlenecks are points in a system that prevent an application from scaling. This can be compared to trying to drive morning peak traffic over one lane. No matter how fast the cars can drive, the lane is a bottleneck and causes a traffic jam. While some bottlenecks are caused by a genuine lack of resource or an intentional act to slow things down, most unintended bottlenecks (software especially) are just a result of bad design.

With respect to design, cloud-based services provide software developers with some additional options in the design of good software that is free of unintended bottlenecks. The cloud is not a silver bullet though. Applications will not automatically be free of unintended bottlenecks once 'deployed' on the cloud, not on either an IaaS or even a PaaS based deployment. For example, a bottleneck existing on an overloaded database server will persist even if deployed on the cloud as long as the fundamental architectural design of the application does not change (see Figure 4.4).

To truly reap the benefit of the cloud in terms of bottleneck prevention, developers need to consider the type of bottleneck and the nature of the process involved in order to arrive at a design that possibly mitigates the unintended bottleneck. In the "horizontal scalability" section we already saw a few potential general bottlenecks such as the file system. In this section we'll be looking specifically at finding bottlenecks within your own application.

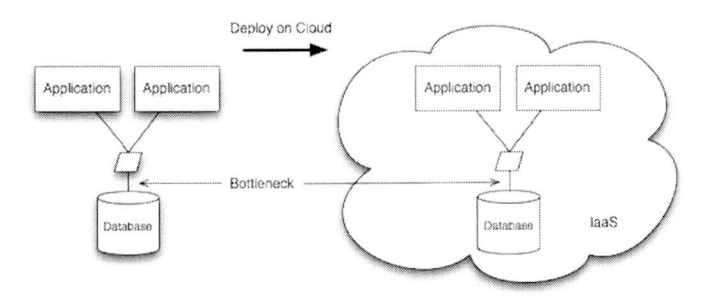

Figure 4.4

Types of Bottlenecks

There are several approaches to classifying bottlenecks. The system administrator's approach will involve the use of capacity planning tools (i.e., netstat[9], sar[10], lockstat[11], top[12] to identify common bottlenecks occurring in low-level resources such as disk I/Os, network interfaces, processing power and memory. Such an approach will typically uncover hardware or environmental bottlenecks that are resolvable with hardware-level resource changes (i.e. add more resource, load-balance).

While this helps unblock low-level bottlenecks, software level flaws in design or implementation may not be immediately visible. For example, a memory bottleneck discovered via sar may be caused by a memory-intensive activity that so happens to reside in a high-volume software process. A different approach that can unravel this memory-intensive activity will allow the developer to consider if the activity is valid or avoidable in light of user imperatives and derive better, less expensive solutions that involve better design rather than brute hardware investments.

---

[9] http://www.faqs.org/docs/linux_network/x-087-2-iface.netstat.html
[10] http://pagesperso-orange.fr/sebastien.godard/
[11] http://www.unix.com/man-page/opensolaris/1m/lockstat/
[12] http://linux.about.com/od/commands/l/blcmdl1_top.htm

The approach of a PHP developer with access to the cloud can be very different. As cloud services can be used as part of a design change to prevent bottlenecks, developers should be much more interested in identifying bottlenecks at a higher level, within the flow of a software process. For us PHP-ers, Xdebug allows us to do that. Since most of the software and components we deal with are open source, profiling can be far-reaching, comprehensive and detailed.

Using Xdebug Profiler to Identify Bottlenecks

The Xdebug[13] profiler's "cachegrind" output can be converted to a visual representation using xdebugtoolkit[14] or some other profiling tool[15] to produce a dot graph similar to that in Figure 4.5. Figure 4.5 is a process-execution dot visualization of the non-distributed PictureMe application.

This is the first instance where the sample PictureMe application is referred; many of our examples are within the context of this application (read the Introduction for more information). We'll touch on this application in more detail later on to show the use of cloud-based services in practice. For now, this graph shows an example of a bottleneck occurring in the execution of the putPicture function highlighted in red by xdebugtoolkit. To produce this visualization with your script, you'll need Xdebug installed and enabled on your PHP environment. You'll also need to enable the profiler and specify the profiler output directory as per the following directives within php.ini:

```
xdebug.profiler_enable=1
xdebug.profiler_output_dir=/tmp
```

With the profiler turned on, all you have to do is to execute the script that you wish to profile. The profiling output will be available in the form of "cachegrind.out.[process_id/dir_crc32_hash]" files within the profiler-output directory specified. To visualize the contents of these files, use this command to create a dot-graph visualization with xdebugtoolkit and dot:

---

[13] http://xdebug.org/
[14] http://code.google.com/p/xdebugtoolkit/
[15] http://www.xdebug.org/docs/profiler

Cloud Architecture ▪ 47

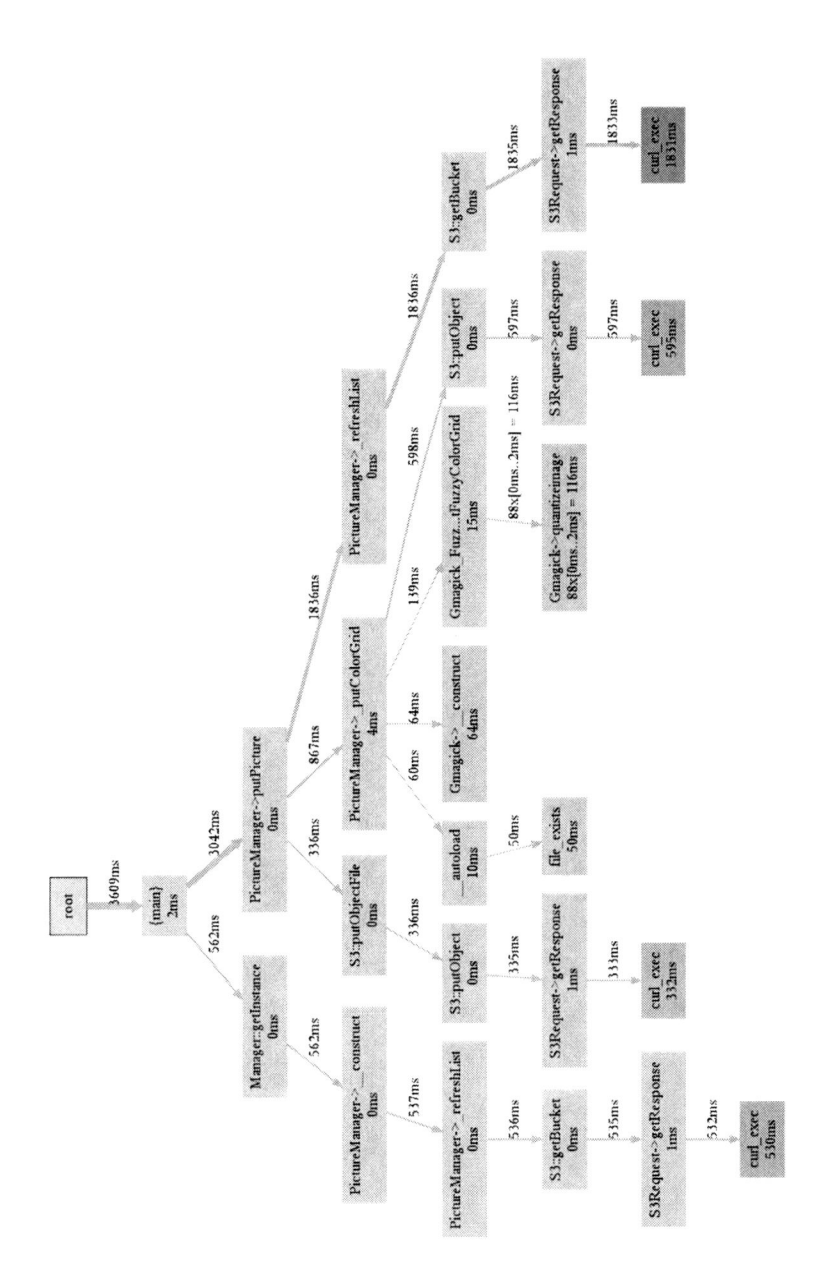

Figure 4.5

```
$ ./cg2dot.py cachegrind.out.[process_id/dir_crc32_hash] |
    dot -Tpng -o [visualization_name].png
```

Circumventing Bottlenecks with the Cloud

Once we have identified a bottleneck, we should analyze the function causing the bottleneck to see if it might be due to a design or implementation flaw. If it is not, we can consider if cloud-based tools or others can be used to prevent the bottleneck. To this end, the thought process flowchart in Figure 4.6 may help.

The straightforward case will be where the cloud does offer a better alternative to resolve the bottleneck. In such a situation, adopting the cloud will be a viable path. For example, where a cloud-based database provides instant scalability versus the traditional, bottleneck-causing, sub-optimal relational database. If there are no straightforward alternatives that the cloud can offer in circumventing the bottleneck, we'll need to consider the user imperatives.

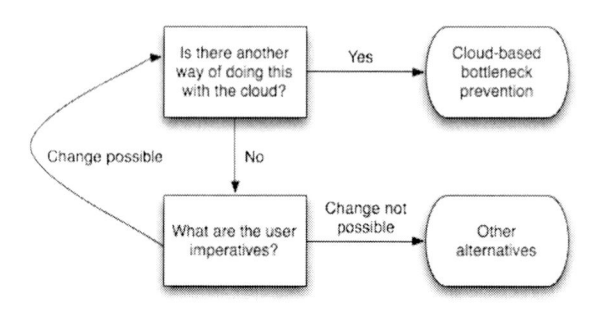

Figure 4.6

For example, Figure 4.5 shows that a likely bottleneck exists within the putPicture function. Further analysis into the code will identify the color-grid generation algorithm of the function as the resource-intensive portion of the function that had caused the bottleneck. (To be fair, the algorithm is doing quite a lot of things depending on the desired level of precision.) Chapter 5 explains the color-grid generation algorithm in further detail. For now, just imagine one of those software programs that turns a photo into a (much simpler) mosaic.

If it is not possible to make the algorithm faster, we then consider the user imperatives with regards to color-grid generation by doing a self Q&A:

Question 1: Is the color grid of a picture absolutely essential? Yes, the color grid is essential to allow precision color searching and this is a feature we are not willing to let go.

Question 2: Is there an absolute need to generate the color grid when the user places a picture on PictureMe? The color grid does not need to be generated immediately while the user places a picture on PictureMe. The user has no direct use of the color grid at all and is generally not interested in viewing it. It is used by the PictureMe application internally to cater for picture searching.

The second question opens up a new viable path in our quest to avoid the bottleneck. Since it is not imperative for the user to view the color grid or even know if it is generated at all, we can allow the user to bypass the color grid generation by delegating the task to an asynchronous process that runs somewhere else. The process that generates the color grid should not be fighting for resources with the user-facing putPicture function in a situation of resource deficiency. Even better, the task of generating the color grid for a picture can be placed on a message queue and be processed by elastically generated workers. This approach is in fact detailed in Chapter 5, where we see how cloud-based servers that can be created and destroyed by web service calls allow us to implement a fully elastic solution to prevent the bottleneck with color grid generation.

Nevertheless, what we have gone through with regards to software profiling and higher-level scrutiny on user imperatives is true of all development endeavors, not just those involving the cloud. What the cloud can bring to the table, if it is not the only way of resolving a bottleneck, is choice. Developers can consider the cloud along with other solutions (hardware, etc.) in light of factors such as cost, maintainability, complexity, security and durability.

Abstraction

The next architectural topic we discuss is abstraction. Abstraction is a very powerful concept that spans mathematics, psychology, philosophy, language, art and of course, computer science. One could argue that such ubiquity is due to how it is so closely related to the way humans perceive and think about the world.

In this section, we discuss abstraction in terms of the most [common way it is] achieved within an object-oriented language such as PHP, [by declaring me]thods within an abstract class (It's possible to achieve [this using interfac]es instead of abstract classes. Generally in abstraction [it is preferred t]hat abstract classes are used, because there is always some [functionality share]d across all implementations, and an abstract class allows the im[plementatio]n of such shared functionality.). The abstract class will never be instanti[ated, b]ut instead serves as a contract for other extending classes that will implement concrete solutions. The key is that the methods declared in the abstract class define an interface to client objects that will not change, no matter how the underlying implementation changes.

When developing applications, the approach to abstraction that we had just discussed is a good way to cope with change. For parts of an application that could change, such as the portion that depends on the underlying architecture of the system, it is a good idea to create an abstraction layer.

Consider for example, a situation where you have a single database server that you wish to scale when load on the server becomes heavy. There are several ways to do it; you can either use a SaaS-based database that lives on the cloud with scalability managed by the provider; or you can manage scalability yourself by creating a replication setup where one master server replicates data to slave servers, which in turn helps deal with read-only queries.

Either way, it is likely that the way to talk to the database will change. Imagine the situation where there is no database-abstraction layer: your application will require painful changes wherever the application uses the database. With a database-abstraction layer however, things become so much more manageable as only the underlying class that implements the abstract database class needs to be changed. Similar concepts and advantages apply to other infrastructure- or platform-dependent aspects of your applications, such as sessions and file systems.

Abstractions should not place a toll on development cost if it is incorporated early on in a project. Many libraries incorporate the concept of abstraction in their APIs to help clients adapt usage of the library to their needs. The SimpleCloud[16] API for example is an effort to abstract the services of various cloud providers in a consistent way. It abstracts file storage, document storage and simple queue services into

---

[16] http://www.simplecloud.org/

abstract classes and provides vendor-specific implementations that deal with specialized details.

Lastly, abstraction by definition involves a certain degree of generalization. It is important to realize that there are often possible details that need to be excluded when abstracting; abstracted systems generally use common denominator features. We'll have to understand and weigh the trade-offs involved with exclusion of a certain specialized feature versus the interoperability and re-usability achieved. And sometimes these trade-offs can be circumvented by extensible design.

Abstraction is indeed a very powerful concept in software languages. Besides being a means to cope with change, it is also a way to manage complexity and improve productivity. Developers can for example make use of abstracted libraries that had been implemented to speed up development. Nevertheless, knowledge of the underlying implementation to a reasonable extent while still using abstractions to speed things up can be practically useful. Further discussion perhaps is best left to a book on software design.

For cloud providers in general, abstraction means that competition becomes harder. If it becomes easier to switch cloud vendors because of abstraction layers, then they are going to have to compete not in offering unique features, but in providing the best possible functionality with the best possible service.

At the time of writing we have deemed all the off-the-shelf abstraction layers to be not mature enough to use in our book. However, we recommend that in your application's architecture, you build your own levels of abstraction so that you will become less vendor dependent and can reap the benefits mentioned in this section.

Multi-Tenancy

The final architectural topic we look at is multi-tenancy. Multi-tenancy deals with having multiple customers ('tenants') use the same application. This is a concept used in Software as a Service setup. Take Gmail for example: Google's e-mail platform[17] hosts millions of users.

Building multi-tenant applications can be done in a number of ways. Let's look at the most common ones.

---

[17] http://gmail.com

Separate Applications, Separate Databases

The easiest architecture to deal with is one in which you have a separate application and a separate database per customer. There is no risk of mixing up data from two customers, but the disadvantage is that you have to maintain many different installations of your software and database. This can be cumbersome with upgrades, maintenance and monitoring. Typically you will give every customer their own URL, or you use a single url but redirect them to their own application based on the login.

One Application, Separate Databases

A good alternative is to have all users use the same application, but switch databases depending on which customer they belong to. This is a good way of solving the maintenance issue. You only have one codebase to worry about, but the data is still kept securely separate. A disadvantage might be that in this scenario it's harder to customize the application for a particular customer, but with Software as a Service this isn't a common scenario anyway. An advantage is that it's relatively easy to roll out updates to the software, but keep in mind that you need to patch all the databases too.

In general we can state that in most cases this 'one application, separate databases' is a very good approach.

Separate Applications, One Database

The inverse architecture is one in which each user has their own version of the software, but all data is stored in a single, master database. It is very important to be able to separate the data of each tenant in the database, which can be tricky.

This scenario does not offer a lot of advantages so it's generally not recommended.

One Application, One Database

On the other end of the spectrum we have the ultimate multi-tenancy, in which everything is one big application. For applications where there is a lot of sharing between users and there is no real sense of groups of users (companies), this may be a good approach. A general social network may typically employ this model, but a service offering social networks to companies where each of them have an individual private network would be better off with one of the other models.

Advanced Approaches

As your multi-tenant software-service project matures, you may want to consider more advanced architectures. A common advanced architecture is one in which you have a group of tenants use one instance of your application. This 'partitioning' of tenants can be done based on region, company size or any other relevant property of your customer base.

The advantage of partitioning the application is that you still have the benefit of not having to maintain an individual installation per customer, but with the flexibility to separate groups of users when it makes sense. A very big customer with hundreds of users may get its own instance whereas 100 smaller customers with five users each may all use a single instance of the application. Using a bit of DNS magic, you can make this completely transparent to the end user.

Another advantage of having a partitioned customer base is that you can roll out updates to multiple clients simultaneously (as in the 'one application' scenario), but not all of them at once. Software as a Service providers use this to roll out updates to, for example, 10% of their customers, collecting feedback and then rolling it out to their other customers.

Whatever model you choose, it's important to make the decision a part of your architecture, as it will have consequences for the way you build the application.

Chapter 5

Working with Popular Cloud Infrastructures

Amazon's Cloud

Amazon Web Services (See Figure 5.1) is highly notable as a cloud infrastructure provider because of the very innovative ways in which it has packaged the enormous capacity underlying this infrastructure. Although there are many areas that can be improved (e.g. language-specific libraries that are designed to take advantage of language-specific features; more functionalities in the Web Management Console), the existing product line that wraps the infrastructure is diverse and truly provides a convenient set of tools to work with.

There are many possible uses for Amazon's cloud. Here, we'll focus on using it for cloud-based web applications from the perspective of PHP developers. In this sense, what we are looking to do is to move various parts of our web application stack on the left side of Figure 5.1 to the cloud on the right. So instead of storing images, videos and other objects in the file system, we store them on the cloud. Batch-processing and other heavy-duty computing functionalities are also performed on the cloud. The most significant benefit, of course, is that the cloud's capacity is theoretically limitless as compared to that of local servers. What this means is that we do not have to worry about the turnaround time and cost involved in hardware scaling. We can

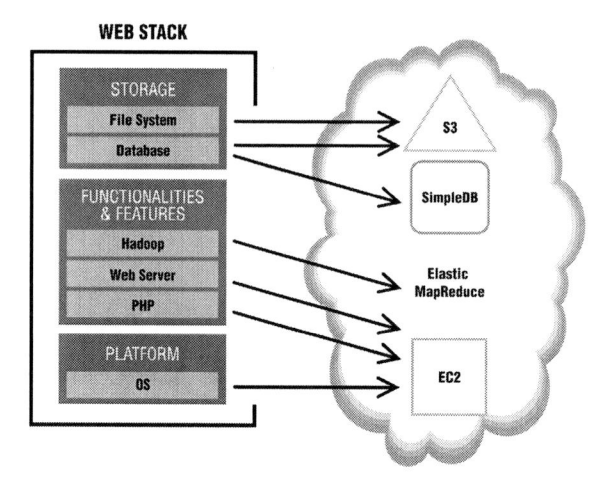

Figure 5.1

also code in new ways, making use of the vast amount of computing resources to do really cool stuff.

Amazon's S3, CloudFront, EC2 and Elastic MapReduce

Amazon's S3, CloudFront, EC2 and MapReduce make the setting up of a powerful, scalable, on-demand, geographically optimized web application environment easy and cheap. EC2 (Elastic Compute Cloud) allows developers to start instances of servers (called Amazon Machine Images) and control them via a web service interface. S3 provides storage on the cloud. Geographically optimized distribution of S3 objects is easily achieved via CloudFront while volume-heavy processing can be performed in a flexible manner with Elastic MapReduce.

A lot of interesting things can be done with these cloud services. One can shoot off MapReduce processing with parallel background scripts on Elastic MapReduce and use EC2 to run scripts and applications that interact with the end user. Similarly, S3 can be used as a file storage for disk backups or as public image or video storage. The commodity pricing is a good deal and the natural growth in computing abundance provides a good downward weight on resource pricing.

PictureMe: the Cloud Application

We will explore the Amazon cloud by building a picture manager application, which we first introduced in the introduction to this book. The application allows the end-user to upload, list, view and delete pictures. It also allows the end user to search for pictures by specifying colors that appear on these pictures. The entire application, including storage and indexing processes, lives on the cloud. We won't be showing the complete application code in this book, but we encourage you to download the sample code[1] for this book. We will be taking relevant snippets from this code to demonstrate our cloud usage.

We shall first build the core features of the application (upload, list, view and delete) using S3, CloudFront and EC2 before going on to use Elastic MapReduce to build the color index that caters for color searching.

Requirements

There are a few things you need to follow this section.

- Register an Amazon AWS account[2] with access to S3, CloudFront (optional), EC2 and Elastic MapReduce
- Don Schonknecht's Amazon S3 PHP class[3]
- cURL
- The S3Fox plug-in[4] for Firefox
- The Amazon EC2 API Tools[5]
- The GMagick PHP extension[6]

---

[1] http://cloudphp.net/downloads/book_samplecode.zip
[2] https://aws-portal.amazon.com/gp/aws/developer/registration/index.html
[3] http://code.google.com/p/amazon-s3-php-class/
[4] https://addons.mozilla.org/en-US/firefox/addon/3247/
[5] http://developer.amazonwebservices.com/connect/entry.jspa?externalID=351
[6] http://www.php.net/manual/en/book.gmagick.php

- The tokyo_tyrant PHP extension[7]

To install the PHP extensions, you'll have to first install their dependencies. Instructions to do so are available on their respective project pages (see the footnotes). Optionally, you'll find that a VM with Hadoop installed is useful as a sandbox for trying out MapReduce locally before running it on Amazon. We'll look at this subsequently.

Storing Pictures in S3

In Simple Storage Service, files are stored within buckets. Metaphorically speaking, S3 buckets are quite similar to real-life buckets: they are used to store stuff. You can store similar items in a bucket or you can store different types of items. They are not entirely the same though and this is where we enter the realm of "cloud-physics"; S3 buckets have a limitless size (or no size, you philosophers). Theoretically, you can store any number of objects on it and it will grow automatically to accommodate your needs. Each object though can only be 5 GB at most.

We first start by creating an S3 bucket to place our pictures. This bucket will form a globally unique namespace in which to locate our pictures. Start S3Fox with the appropriate credentials and click on the Create Directory (somehow, the creators of S3Fox decided to use this term) icon. Give it a good name that is not already used and we shall have a bucket. Donovan Schonknecht's S3 class is an excellent PHP tool to do all sorts of things with the S3 cloud. For example, to place pictures into the bucket, our PictureManager class makes use of a composed S3 instance ($this->_storage) as is shown below:

```
if ($this->_storage->putObjectFile($pictureFile, BUCKET, $pictureName, S3::
    ACL_PUBLIC_READ)) {
  if ($this->_putColorGrid($pictureName, $pictureFile)) {
    $this->_refreshList();
    return 'Picture stored successfully.';
  } else {
    return 'Problem occurred in creating color grid.';
  }
}
```

---
[7]http://www.php.net/manual/en/book.tokyo-tyrant.php

When calling the putObjectFile() method, we have to specify the file to be placed, the bucket and the name of the file. S3::ACL_PUBLIC_READ specifies that the object is publicly available. Objects can be made private (which is the default by the way), publicly readable or even publicly readable and writable.

When successfully executed, a message is returned that will subsequently be displayed by the presentational counterpart index.php. We'll look at _putColorGrid later. For now, let's check out the _refreshList() method, which can be seen here:

```
private function _refreshList()
{
   try {
      $this->_pictureList = $this->_storage->getBucket(BUCKET, null, null,
         MAX_PICTURES);
   } catch (Exception $e) {
      echo $e->getMessage();
   }

   if ($this->_pictureList !== false) {
      usort($this->_pictureList, array('PictureManager', 'pictureCompare'));
   }
}
```

The method is called whenever the state of the bucket changes (add pictures, delete) to synchronize the list of pictures between PictureManager and the actual S3 bucket. The MAX_PICTURES constant limits the amount of results returned. Since PictureManager limits the number of pictures that can be placed in the bucket by the same constant (in the putPicture() method), this is more of a safety check. Although there is no need for it in this case, the two null parameters can be filled with prefix and delimiter, which are useful for situations where searching and hierarchy are required.

Other examples of interacting with S3 are shown in the source code, mostly similar in usage method but different in purpose. The PHP S3 class encapsulates almost everything a typical web application will require when using the S3 cloud. In the background, it manages the generation of the correct REST HTTP requests to Amazon S3 and the processing of the response. Hence, if further detail is required on any parameter of the PHP S3 methods besides those already commented within the class, we can check the corresponding request documentation on Amazon's S3 Developer

Guide. For example, the Common List Request Parameters page details information on the parameters for the `getBucket()` method.

For the sake of this example application we only store pictures with size of up to 500 kb. Amazon S3 can store objects of up to 5 GB in size but the S3 PHP class can only handle objects of up to 2GB in size on 32 bit systems due to PHP's signed integer limitation. The smallest object size that can be uploaded to S3 is 1 byte, but practically, it is more cost efficient to store larger objects because of the way Amazon charges on PUT requests. Data transfer rates are also relatively faster as well with larger objects because of communication overheads.

Geographical Optimization with CloudFront

When you upload an object on S3, you are able to specify the geographic location of the server that stores the object (with the optional location_constraint parameter). While you may want to choose a specific location in certain cases, most applications that service international users can benefit from the object being within closer geographic proximity. CloudFront allows the developer to do just that. It is essentially a Content Distribution Network (CDN) that is tailored for S3 objects.

With CloudFront, a user from Asia accessing a S3 object in Europe for the first time will trigger a one-time transfer of a copy of the object from the European server to one of the Amazon's servers that resides in Asia. The copy of the object will then be stored in the Asian server. The next time the object is requested from a user in Asia, the object duplicate residing in the Asian server will be delivered to the user instead, speeding up delivery as the object will need to traverse fewer nodes.

It is really easy to enable CloudFront because of its close compatibility with S3. Remember the bucket we created with S3Fox? Now, open S3Fox again, and under Remote View, right click on the bucket we created earlier. Choose Manage Distribution, then click on Create Distribution within the dialog box. You should see the InProgress status within the distribution list for the bucket. Refresh your view after a while and the status should change to Deployed.

Now notice the Domain Name information within the dialog box. The domain name will form part of the URL to access your S3 object via CloudFront. In PictureMe for example, a picture object with the name london.jpg can be publicly accessed via `http://[DOMAIN_NAME]/london.jpg`. This is actually how pictures are shown within

PictureMe where the url is used within the src attribute of an IMG tag. Pictures accessed via the CloudFront domain name will automatically be delivered via the best geographically located server.

CloudFront unfortunately is not a default service but rather another service that you have to activate and subscribe to. It is payable as well, on top of the storage charges that already apply to S3. The good news is that it is rather cheap relatively, compared to the enhanced end-user experience that it delivers, especially for high-traffic international sites.

Amazon's Elastic Compute Cloud

Amazon EC2 doesn't just have a fancy name: the Elastic Compute Cloud does actually place a lot of computing power in the hands of the public at a decently reasonable price. The focus of the ECC is machine creation and management, and the tools available to do this efficiently are growing rapidly.

The ECC is in essence a web service that allows developers to start virtual machines with operating systems via the Internet. These machines can be used to do all kinds of things such as batch processing, video encoding and streaming, as well as more conventional things like web or database hosting. Depending on what you will be doing, there are hundreds of AMIs (Amazon Machine Images) available that are specialized for specific tasks.

PictureMe, for example, can be placed on an instance of a standard Linux-based AMI with Apache and PHP. One such AMI that is publicly available is the one identified by Amazon as ami-2e5fba47.

The EC2 documentation describes a typical process of starting an instance and controlling it, as well as the generation of the private key required for authenticating access to the instance. You should install Amazon EC2's API Tools package on the machine that will manage the creation of instances. This package can be obtained from the Amazon EC2 Resource Center[8]. For the purpose of going along with this example, you may install it on your local machine if you're comfortable with that. Installation involves unzipping the zip file to a desired location and the setting of the following environment variables:

---

[8] http://developer.amazonwebservices.com/connect/entry.jspa?externalID=351&categoryID=88

62 ■ Working with Popular Cloud Infrastructures

```
$ export EC2_HOME=[path-to-tools]
$ export PATH=$PATH:$EC2_HOME/bin
$ export EC2_PRIVATE_KEY=~/.ec2/[private_key].pem
$ export EC2_CERT=~/.ec2/[certificate].pem
$ export EC2_URL=https://[service_endpoint]
```

The private key and certificate are obtained by logging into your account[9]. Then, go to X.509 `Certificates > Create a New Certificate`. Save the certificate and private key in a hidden `.ec2` directory, which you should create in your home directory. The service_endpoint, on the other hand, can be obtained from a list created by running the `ec2-describe-regions` command. You should specify a service_endpoint that is geographically optimal for your needs. Otherwise, the instance will be created in Eastern US by default.

To try PictureMe on the ECC, start an instance of ami-2e5fba47 by using the `ec2-run-instances` command bundled in Amazon EC2's API Tools package.

```
# ec2-run-instances  ami-2e5fba47
```

To obtain information about the started instance, do:

```
# ec2-describe-instances [instance_id]
```

This should return something similar to the following:

```
RESERVATION r-8932c31d 9287659495 default
INSTANCE [instance_id] [AMI] [hostname] ip-10-189-39-163.ec2.internal [state]
    gsg-keypair 0 m1.small
2008-03-21T16:19:25+0000us-east-1a
```

Some of the notable elements include `instance_id`, AMI, hostname and the state of the instance, which should be running if the instance is successfully started. We then place the PictureMe files onto the instance as follows:

```
# scp -i [private_key_file] * root@[hostname]:/var/www/html/
```

---

[9] http://aws.amazon.com

`private_key_file` is the `private_key` you generate for authentication and `hostname` is the hostname of the machine as described by the `ec2-describe-instances` command. Once the files are placed, the PictureMe application can be accessed publicly via the internet at: `http://`**`[hostname]`**

The EC2 is a very powerful tool, and good utilization of its strength relies heavily on the creativity of the developer to manipulate the cloud, i.e. to automate and balance the creation of new instances and to create masters of instances and other forms of hierarchy. Meanwhile, there are also concepts such as Elastic IPs to support convenient dynamic server instantiation and termination. Elastic IPs allow the mapping of servers to an Internet-routable static IP address via an API. This way, servers behind an Elastic IP are interchangeable on the background without changing the Elastic IP, and the hassle of managing IP changes can be avoided.

The diagram in Figure 5.2 sums up the PictureMe web-application ecosystem at this point. The end user interacts with the application that is hosted on EC2. Pictures are stored on S3 while CloudFront stores copies of pictures in locations that are closer to the end user. Next up, we'll look at using Elastic MapReduce to perform the data-intensive task of indexing colors of pictures stored by PictureMe.

Searching for Colors

There are many insights that we can gain by considering colors. For example, a search for Manchester football teams will yield more meaningful results if colors close to either primary red or blue are specified, and that certainly makes all the difference.

We can also use information implicit in colors to fulfill our search requirements without additional search support structure. If we want to search for the Victoria line on London's useful tube map, for example, we could search for the light blue color RGB(24, 132, 188) instead of having to set up the vector structures or other means to enable highlighting of the line. With Gmagick, we can highlight search results, as we shall see further on in this section.

More specificity in terms of colors and positions certainly helps too. Consider a situation where we are looking for a red roof in a collection of paintings. Knowing the opacity and location of red occurrences helps in narrowing down the scope of search.

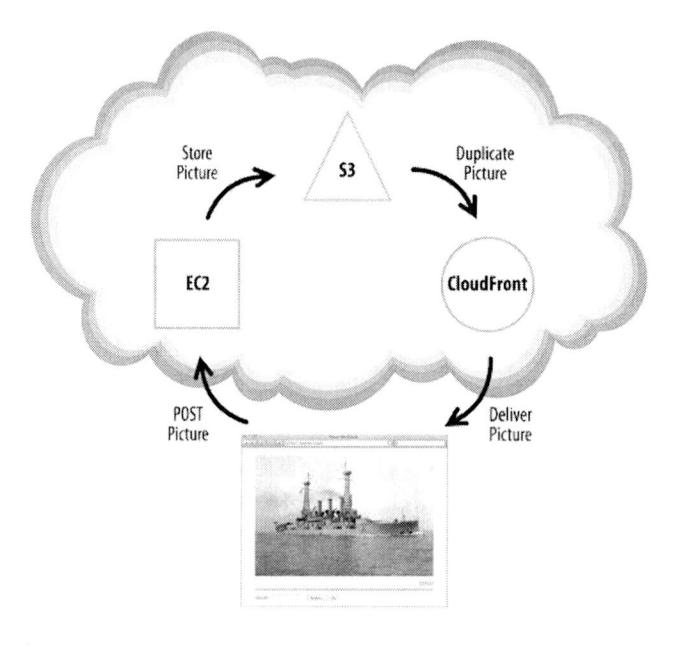

Figure 5.2

The necessary challenge with enhancing specificity is the one ultimately latent in all human endeavors, that of resource constrain. A typical image usually contains millions of pixels. Storing and indexing a large amount of images is resource intensive depending on the quantization level. While computing resources in the domain of individual servers had been intensive and will continue to increase dramatically, the cloud has presented itself as a practical and available solution for us to do such resource-intensive tasks.

We will use Amazon's Elastic Map/Reduce and PHP to add color-searching capability to the PictureMe application. The application will allow flexible definition of search specificity by adjusting the size of a search "cell", the pixel size of a segment within any image that can be searched. The application can be scaled to support finer cell sizes and larger sets of images by riding on the elasticity of the Amazon MapReduce cloud.

MapReduce

MapReduce is a programming model to process large data sets with a distributed and parallelized cluster of computers. A pool of input data is partitioned into smaller chunks, and these are allocated to a particular machine within the cluster. Data to be processed via MapReduce has to be key/value pairs. Developers using a MapReduce setup typically write the Map function and the Reduce function.

The Map function takes in a key/value pair, performs some processing, then outputs an intermediate key/value pair. The kind of processing depends on what the developer wants to achieve. For our color-searching application, for example, we provide as input to the Mapper function key/value pairs of locations and the color at that location. The Mapper function then outputs intermediate key/value pairs of colors and the locations that contain a particular color. This key/value pair is then used as input to the Reducer function, which merges all intermediate values associated with the same intermediate key. In our case, the Reducer groups together the output of Mappers to output a key/value pair of color and all locations globally within the initial data set that has the particular color. What do we achieve from this whole MapReduce job? Well, we obtain an index of all available colors and their corresponding location. We could do it very quickly because work was done in parallel by various machines instead of sequentially by a single machine.

Hadoop's Map Reduce

A popular way to create a MapReduce cluster is via the Hadoop framework. Amazon's Elastic MapReduce is based on Hadoop MapReduce. Hadoop MapReduce is part of the Hadoop project which covers a series of other helpful tools along the theme of distributed computing, i.e., a data-collection system (Chukwa), a distributed database (HBase), a distributed-file system (HDFS), a data-warehouse infrastructure (Hive), a high-level data-flow language (Pig) and a coordination service (ZooKeeper).

The setup of a Hadoop MapReduce cluster involves the installation of Hadoop on all machines involved. Then, we'll have to designate the masters: a Namenode machine and another JobTracker machine. Then come the slaves: DataNode and Task-Tracker machines. These allocations are performed via a lot of configuration and there are a host of other considerations such as ACLs, storage paths, memory usage and limits. Well, you might end up more of a Hadoop specialist than a PHP developer after going through a full and precise Hadoop setup. Managers, on the other hand, should be aware of the resources required to set up and maintain a Hadoop cluster.

The good thing is, Amazon's Elastic MapReduce offering encapsulates a lot of these details, presenting a minimal interface to get you running quickly. Coupled with PHP's strength in this area, the pair combines well as a feasible and accessible platform for large amounts of data processing without the enormous time and hardware cost.

The Color Indexing Architecture

Figure 5.3 explains how the color indexing and searching ecosystem works. We add a `_putColorGrid()` method to PictureManager that utilizes the `getFuzzyColorGrid()` method of Gmagick_Fuzzy (which we will look at later) and some other core functions of Gmagick to generate a color-grid representation of an image. For every picture image that is uploaded to the BUCKET, a file containing the color-grid representation of the picture is uploaded to a COLOR_GRID_BUCKET. Color-grid files stored within this bucket will be used as input to the `mapper.php`.

The MapReduce side of things will be responsible to churn out an indexed table of all available colors and their corresponding location within the S3 storage. This indexed data will be stored in a COLOR_INDEX_BUCKET that will be accessed by Search-

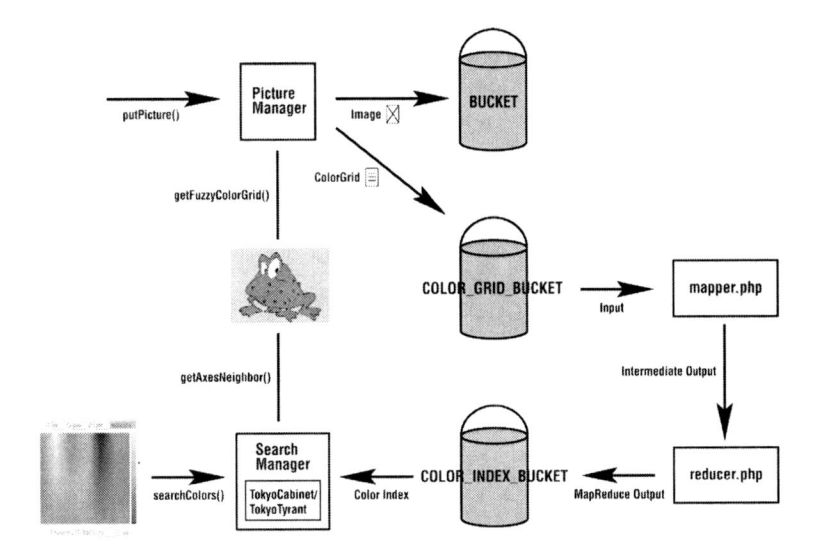

Figure 5.3

Manager when an index update is performed. TokyoCabinet/TokyoTyrant is used as a fast local storage of the color index. We provide a precise color picker to the user, and allow the user to also specify a search proximity. The `getFuzzyNeighbors()` method in `Gmagick_FriendlyPixel` returns all colors that are within the specified 3D proximity of the chosen color pixel.

The Color Grid

"One picture is worth ten thousand words", so says Fred. R. Barnard. The phrase is literally true when it comes to pixel representation of images, but this depends on the complexity of the image in terms of colors. In the field of computer graphics, RGB, one of the most popular colorspace programs, can represent up to 16.5 million colors to account for differing opacity, allowing visualization of precise light intensity, tones and shadows that would have made Vermeer envious. We shall make use of this immense colorspace to construct the color grid of our color search engine.

Color searching at the pixel level can be an enormous task in a reasonably sized image repository. A typical picture will have at least one million pixels. Here's where color grid helps. Instead of considering every pixel within an image, we divide the image into rows and columns of cells, each cell being of a fixed size. The colors in each cell are also quantized to obtain a single representative color of the cell. Figure 5.4 shows what a color grid of an image will look like.

Figure 5.4

The `PictureManager` contains a method that creates this color grid using an extended version of Gmagick called `Gmagick_Fuzzy`. `Gmagick_Fuzzy` is a PHP userland class that is created for the purpose of this example and is available in the source code that accompanies this book. Gmagick Fuzzy inherits all attributes and methods of Gmagick but adds an additional method called `getFuzzyColorGrid()`.

Besides the creation of the color grid, the `PictureManager` also places a file that is representative of this color grid on a defined color grid bucket on S3. Let's take a look at the following code:

```
protected function _putColorGrid($pictureName, $pictureFile)
{
    try {
        $fgm = new Gmagick_Fuzzy($pictureFile);
        $colorGrid = $fgm->getFuzzyColorGrid(CELL_SIZE);
```

```
      $pictureColorGrid = '';
      foreach ($colorGrid as $rowKey => $colorRow) {
         foreach ($colorRow as $colKey => $colorColumn) {
            $pictureColorGrid .= $pictureName.'['.$rowKey.','.$colKey.']'.chr
               (9).substr($colorColumn, 3).PHP_EOL;
         }
      }

      if ($this->_storage->putObject($pictureColorGrid,
         COLOR_GRID_BUCKET, $pictureName,
         S3::ACL_PUBLIC_READ, array(), 'text/plain')) {

         return true;
      } else {
         return false;
      }
   } catch (Exception $e) {
      return false;
   }
}
```

A `Gmagick_Fuzzy` object is instantiated, passing in the `$pictureFile` to the constructor as we would do with the normal Gmagick class. Next, on the `$fgm` object, we call getFuzzyColorGrid, passing in the desired CELL_SIZE, which is the size of the rectangular cell in pixels. The getFuzzyCollorGrid method is detailed in the snippet below:

```
public function getFuzzyColorGrid($gridSize)
{
   $colorGrid = array();
   for ($i = 0; $i < $this->getImageWidth(); $i += $gridSize) {
      for ($j = 0; $j < $this->getImageHeight(); $j += $gridSize) {
         $cropped = clone $this;
         $histogram = $cropped->cropImage($gridSize, $gridSize, $i, $j)
                     ->quantizeImage(1, Gmagick::COLORSPACE_RGB, 0, false,
                        false)
                     ->getImageHistogram();
         $colorGrid[$i][$j] = $histogram[0]->getColor();
      }
   }
   return $colorGrid;
}
```

getFuzzyColorGrid() is an extended Gmagick method that chops the image into small sections, quantizes these smaller sections to a single color and returns an array of colors of all these smaller sections.

Back in the _putColorGrid method in PictureManager, we subsequently create a color-grid string. We format the color-grid information in pairs of location and color. Each line will denote a pair of location and color, starting with the top left of the image to the bottom right. This color-grid string is then placed in a COLOR_GRID_BUCKET on S3. Files in this bucket will be used as input to our mapper function, which we'll look at next.

The Mapper

Remember our earlier description of the Mapper function when we discussed MapReduce? Here's what the implementation in PHP looks like. Our map function receives input (key/value pairs of location/color) allocated to it by Hadoop and performs some reorganizing and formatting before passing it on to the reducer.

```
#!/usr/bin/php
<?php

while (($line = fgets(STDIN)) !== false) {
    $line = trim($line);
    list($location,$color) = explode(chr(9), $line);
    if (empty($colorArray["{$color}"])) {
        $colorArray["{$color}"] = $location;
    } else {
        $colorArray["{$color}"] = implode('|', array($colorArray["{$color}"],
            $location));
    }
}
foreach($colorArray as $color => $locations) {
    echo $color, chr(9), $locations.PHP_EOL;
}
?>
```

Input sent to the map function is always in key/value pairs, with location as the key and the color at that location as the value. Here's a sample snippet of input lines that is typically received by the mapper:

```
Image001.jpg[0,0]   (72,71,85)
Image001.jpg[0,10]  (76,65,79)
Image001.jpg[0,20]  (75,69,82)
Image001.jpg[0,30]  (68,62,72)
Image001.jpg[0,40]  (64,62,77)
Image001.jpg[0,50]  (66,60,77)
Image001.jpg[0,60]  (72,56,74)
Image001.jpg[0,70]  (68,53,72)
Image001.jpg[0,80]  (68,53,72)
...
```

By default, Hadoop will order the input lines by ascending binary value before allocating the input to the mapper function. The mapper takes each line and explodes it to obtain the color and location data. A colorArray is used to store a list of locations that has a particular color, with the color as the key. The mapper adds to this colorArray for each line it encounters, building up the list of locations for a particular color. After looking at all the inputs, the mapper outputs each item in the colorArray, indicating each color and the corresponding locations as key/value pairs:

```
(64,62,77)   Image001.jpg[0,40]
(66,60,77)   Image001.jpg[0,50]
(68,53,72)   Image001.jpg[0,70]|Image001.jpg[0,80]
(68,62,72)   Image001.jpg[0,30]
(72,56,74)   Image001.jpg[0,60]
(72,71,85)   Image001.jpg[0,0]
(75,69,82)   Image001.jpg[0,20]
(76,65,79)   Image001.jpg[0,10]
...
```

This intermediate output will then be used by the reducer to build a storage-wide index of color locations.

The Reducer

The reduce function merges together all locations from the intermediate output with the same intermediate color key. Here is the code for our reducer:

```
#!/usr/bin/php
<?php
```

```php
while (($line = fgets(STDIN)) !== false) {
    $line = trim($line);
    list($color, $locations) = explode(chr(9), $line);
    if (empty($wholeColorArray["{$color}"])) {
        $wholeColorArray["{$color}"] = $locations;
    } else {
        $wholeColorArray["{$color}"] = implode('|', array($wholeColorArray["{
            $color}"], $locations));
    }
}
foreach($wholeColorArray as $color => $locations) {
    echo $color, chr(9), $locations.PHP_EOL;
}
?>
```

Similarly, a `wholeColorArray` is used to store a list of color/locations pair, but this time the array stores color/locations that are representative of the whole PictureMe S3 storage, not just a chunk of partitioned inputs. We do the same as with Mapper to output all the colors and locations available to the final output bucket of the MapReduce process.

Hint: Notice at the beginning of the map and reduce code how we indicate to Hadoop streaming the executable that we wish to use to execute the script (`#!/usr/bin/php`).

Sandboxing on a VM with Apache Hadoop

The Apache Hadoop VM is useful as a test environment for your MapReduce application before deploying it on the cloud. It provides a safe space for you to experiment with, and most importantly, do so in a cost-free manner. We shall go through the process of running the PictureMe indexing MapReduce application to illustrate the use of this great tool. Here, we use Yahoo's Hadoop VM[10].

Make sure you run apt-get on the VM to install PHP with cURL.

First, we transfer the necessary files to the VM using Secure Copy:

```
#scp * hadoop-user@<hadoop_vm_ip>:/home/hadoop-user/Color
```

---

[10] http://p.yimg.com/c/ycs/ydn/hadoop/hadoop-vm-appliance-0-18-0_v1.zip

Make sure you have `mapper.php`, `reducer.php` and some sample input files (color grids) uploaded as well. The source code contains two such input files.

Next, on the VM, we'll need to load the input onto Hadoop's distributed filesystem. Move the input files to a directory, say `Color/colorsource`, within the hadoop-user home directory, then copy the whole directory into the distributed filesystem (HDFS):

```
#hadoop fs -copyFromLocal /home/hadoop-user/Color/colorsource/ colorsource
```

Then make sure the mapper and reducer files can be read and executed:

```
#chmod -R 555 Color
```

With that, you're ready to start:

```
#hadoop jar hadoop/contrib/streaming/hadoop-0.18.0-streaming.jar
   -mapper /home/hadoop-user/Color/mapper.php
   -reducer /home/hadoop-user/Color/reducer.php
   -input colorsource/* -output color-output
```

Make sure the name of the output directory does not already exist within the distributed filesystem. Once the job has been completed, you can retrieve it:

```
#hadoop fs -copyToLocal color-output ./
```

You should be able to see something similar to the following in the files within the `color-output` directory if everything is right:

```
(64,62,77)   Image001.jpg[0,40]|Image001.jpg[0,80]|Image001.jpg[30,50]
(66,60,77)   Image001.jpg[0,50]
```

These key/value pairs will be stored in our local key/value storage, which we will look at shortly.

The hadoop fs is the tool to use to interact with the distributed filesystem. For a list of available commands, do `#hadoop fs -help`.

Creating the JobFlow on Elastic MapReduce

Once the MapReduce application has been tested and verified on the sandbox VM, we shall then move it to the cloud. Since we already have our input color-grid file in the COLOR_GRID_BUCKET on S3, doing this is really just a matter of moving the mapper and reducer to a bucket on S3 (not the bucket that stores the input files though!).

We will use Amazon's AWS Management Console[11] to launch the indexing job flow and to monitor the progress of the job flow. A job flow comprises the map and reduce functions and the input and output involved. We will create a Streaming job flow primarily, using Hadoop's streaming utility to use PHP to run our PHP-based mapper and reducer. Once you're logged in to the "Elastic MapReduce" tab on AWS Management Console, click on the "Create New Job Flow" button. Specify a name for your job flow, say "Color Indexing", and choose "Streaming", then "Continue". Next, enter the following values for the specified parameters:

```
Input Location: s3n://[COLOR_GRID_BUCKET]
Output Location:s3n://[output_location]
Mapper: s3n://[src_storage_bucket]/mapper.php
Reducer: s3n://[src_storage_bucket]/reducer.php
```

The output_location name has to be unused; if you want to use a bucket name that already exists, make sure you delete the bucket first before starting your JobFlow, otherwise it will fail.

Continue to the next section, and you'll be asked to specify the number and type of instances to run. Important in this section is the Advanced Options, where you will be presented with the chance to specify an S3 log path. This log is really useful for debug, development and maintenance use, so do specify a bucket to place this log information.

Once all that is specified and reviewed, start the job and a new row will be created on the Elastic MapReduce console main page. When the state changes to COMPLETED, you will be able to extract the output of the job flow from the output bucket. Make sure that the output location used in the job flow is specified in the COLOR_INDEX_BUCKET of config.inc so that the SearchManager knows that it has to use

---
[11]http://aws.amazon.com/console

this bucket. The index will need to be updated in a suitable interval to account for new pictures stored and other possible changes within the color-grid file.

Updating the Color Index to Local Storage

We will need to use a local key/value store to hold our color locations. As a single image can have millions of pixels and a search range can also be very large, we need a storage mechanism that we can read from and write to in large amounts very quickly to maintain good user experience with the application throughout.

For our case here, TokyoCabinet/TokyoTyrant seems suitable. You can adapt the code to use any other key/value store that you prefer (there are others such as MemcacheDB and Redis), but Tokyo Cabinet is a very efficient library to manage key/-value databases (insert:0.4 sec/1M records, search:0.33 sec/1M records). We will use the tokyo_tyrant PHP extension[12] to interact with the Tokyo Tyrant client library (Tokyo Tyrant is the network interface to Tokyo Cabinet) from within PHP. Brief installation instructions are as follows:

Tokyo Cabinet and Tokyo Tyrant

- Obtain the latest versions of Tokyo Cabinet[13] and Tokyo Tyrant[14], and extract accordingly

- `./configure`

- `make`

- `make install`

tokyo_tyrant Extension

- Obtain the latest version of the tokyo_tyrant extension[15] and extract accordingly

---

[12] http://pecl.php.net/package/tokyo_tyrant/
[13] http://1978th.net/tokyocabinet/
[14] http://1978th.net/tokyotyrant/
[15] http://pecl.php.net/package/tokyo_tyrant/

- phpize
- ./configure
- make
- make install

Make sure you have the right output bucket name in your COLOR_INDEX_BUCKET defined within `config.inc` and your TokyoCabinet/TokyoTyrant server instance started:

```
#ttserver local.tch  (where local.tch is the database name)
```

We retrieve a list of all output indexing files from the output bucket:

```
$indexFiles = $this->_storage->getBucket(COLOR_INDEX_BUCKET);
```

Then, we retrieve each of these files and place the key-value data embedded in each line into our local store, as can be seen below.

```
foreach ($indexFiles as $name => $info) {
   $index = $this->_storage->getObject(COLOR_INDEX_BUCKET, $name);
   $colorLocationsArray = explode(PHP_EOL, $index->body);
   foreach ($colorLocationsArray as $colorLocations) {
      $colorLocations = trim($colorLocations);
      list($color, $locations) = explode(chr(9), $colorLocations);
      if (!empty($locations) && !empty($locations)) {
         $storedColors["{$color}"] = $locations;
      }
   }
   $this->_localStore->put($storedColors);
}
```

Since search requests are made with colors, we can quickly retrieve location information for each color requested by using color as the key in our store.

Handling Search Requests

Search requests on the front-end are handled by the `searchColor()` method of `SearchManager`. This method first filters the RGB color values before instantiating a `Gmagick_FriendlyPixel`.

```
$pixel = Gmagick_FriendlyPixel("rgb({$r},{$g},{$b})");
```

This extended version of Gmagick has a method called `getAxesNeighbor()` that returns all neighbors to the pixel that is within the `$proximity` specified in a 3D colorspace.

```
$neighbors = $pixel->getAxesNeighbor($proximity);
```

The `$proximity` helps in allowing search users to control the scope of the search while conserving color relatedness.

The next step is to retrieve the locations stored in our local storage for each of the colors in the `$neighbors` array. Each location consists of the filename and the position (coordinates) in which the color is found. For each of the locations retrieved, we extract the filename and coordinates of each position within the file. We then use this information to rebuild a file-specific mapping of coordinate positions and searched color on that location that had been found. An example of such a mapping:

```
[vermeer.jpg|0.60767500 1253551071] =>
Array(
    [[70,160]] => (165,171,167)
    [[620,590]] => (167,168,154)
    [[380,460]] => (167,168,160)
    [[260,20]] => (168,167,161)
    [[540,540]] => (168,168,156)
    [[50,60]] => (168,184,173)
    [[490,550]] => (169,172,154)
    [[0,20]] => (169,186,171)
    [[590,350]] => (170,170,162)
    [[550,540]] => (170,172,159)
    [[500,550]] => (170,173,154)
    [[560,560]] => (170,173,154)
)
```

We keep a copy of this mapping for each file in our local store so that we can quickly retrieve it to draw indicators on the image where colors had been found. We'll discuss this in the next section. It is important to note now that the local store is used also for search-result caching as well as color indexing. The value 0.60767500 1253551071 in the above example is essentially a `$searchTime` obtained by using `microtime()` to introduce some uniqueness to this search result. At this point, we index search results as such so that we can be specific when retrieving these search results at a later time:

```php
$searchTime = microtime();
foreach ($neighbors as $neighbor) {
   $locations = $this->_localStore->get('('.implode(',', $neighbor).')');
   if ($locations !== NULL) {
      foreach (explode('|', $locations) as $location) {
         $file = substr($location, 0, strpos($location, '['));
         $position = strstr($location, '[');
         $colorPosition["{$position}"] = '('.implode(',', $neighbor).')'
         $locationColors["{$file}|{$searchTime}"] = $colorPosition;
         $fileColors["{$file}|{$searchTime}"] = serialize($colorPosition);
      }
      $this->_localStore->put($fileColors);
   }
}
if (empty($locationColors)) {
   return false;
} else {
   uasort($locationColors, array('SearchManager', 'locationCompare'));
}
return $locationColors;
```

Finally, before returning the result to the user, we sort it by size as a straightforward way of ranking the search result. This way, images with the most cell positions found for colors in the `$neighbors` array are ranked highest.

```php
uasort($locationColors, array("SearchManager", "locationCompare"));
static function locationCompare($a, $b) {
   if (sizeof($a) == sizeof($b)) {
      return 0;
   }
   return (sizeof($a) > sizeof($b)) ? -1 : +1;
}
```

We then display the $locationColors search results returned to the user. Figure 5.5 is an example of what a search result will look like on the front end.

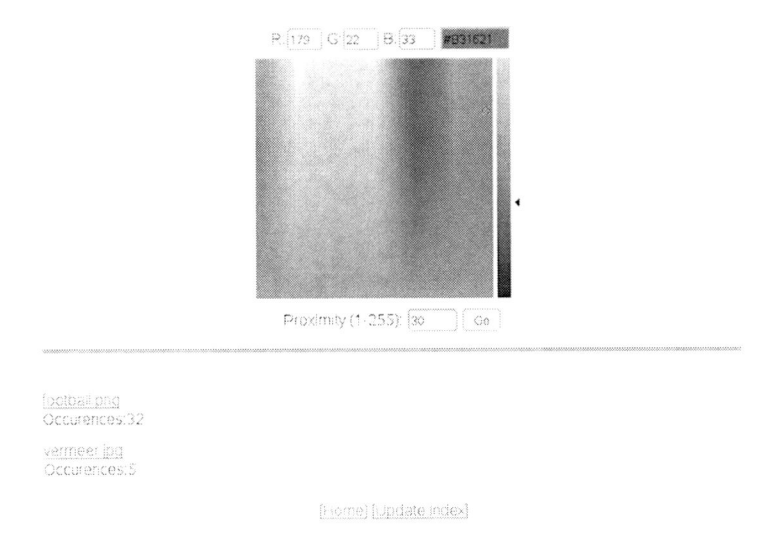

Figure 5.5

Mapping Matching Positions

Remember the microtime-d color positions for specific search results that we placed in the local TokyoCabinet/TokyoTyrant storage? We can use that to draw a series of rectangles around cell positions where search matches are found before returning a result image to the user. First, we retrieve it:

```
$positions = unserialize($this->_localStore->get($pictureSearchResult));
//$pictureSearchResult consists of the file name and the search time
//$pictureSearchResult = "{$fileName}|{$searchTime}"
```

We also instantiate `GmagickDraw` wand object next, using it to add a series of rectangles for each position retrieved:

```
$positionOverlay = new GMagickDraw();
```

```
$positionOverlay->setFillColor('transparent')->setStrokeColor('yellow')->
    setStrokeWidth('2');
foreach ($positions as $position => $color) {
   list($x, $y) = explode(',', rtrim(ltrim($position, '['), ']'));
   $positionOverlay->rectangle($x, $y, $x+CELL_SIZE, $y+CELL_SIZE);
}
```

We then instantiate a `Gmagick` object, passing in the URL of the image to its constructor.

```
list($fileName, $searchTime) = explode('|', $pictureSearchResult);
gmPicture = new Gmagick(STORAGE_RESOURCE_URL.'/'.$fileName);
```

This allows us to manipulate the image in all sorts of ways. Of most interest to us is the ability to draw on the image with the `GmagickDraw` drawing wand created earlier;

```
$gmPicture->drawImage($positionOverlay)
```

Finally, we write the image to a temporary location and return the URL to this location to the front-end;

```
$gmPicture->write('tmp_img/'.$pictureSearchResult); // Ensure write permissions
    on tmp_img
$picture['url'] = './tmp_img/'.$pictureSearchResult;
$picture['name'] = $pictureSearchResult;
return $picture;
```

The result of these sequences of code, all wrapped in `getSearchMatches()` of `PictureManager` can be seen in Figure 5.6, where we display the result of searching RGB (179, 22, 33) with proximity 10.

The result of searching for RGB (179, 22, 33) with proximity 30 is in Figure 5.7.

Automatic Elasticity with Rackspace Cloud

Earlier in Chapter 4, we saw how bottlenecks can be identified and debated whether cloud solutions can help mitigate bottlenecks. We also considered how horizontal scalability can be achieved.

Figure 5.6

Figure 5.7

While automatic horizontal scalability is an implicit feature of PaaS-based clouds, we usually have to manage scalability on our own with IaaS-based clouds.

Rapid elasticity is one of the five NIST characteristics but this does not mean that this elasticity comes automatically. Rackspace Servers, an IaaS solution, for example, comes with server instances with limited capacity. Typically a 1.5 cent per hour server has 256Mb of memory and a 10GB disk size. Although we can resize the memory of a server on-the-run, there is still a maximum limit on the amount of memory that we can allocate.

This section provides an overview of the nooks and crannies involved in taking elasticity in your own hands. It is not exhaustive, but serves more as a starting point for further exploration into deeper elasticity concerns or perhaps highlights the tremendous convenience of PaaS-based cloud such as Rackspace Sites where elasticity is implicit. We are scaling up and down by starting and shutting down server instances instead of just adjusting memory allocation.

The Rackspace Cloud

Rackspace's cloud offering is divided into three main products: Sites, Servers and Files.

Rackspace *Files* is a CDN-enabled, cloud-based file storage service in direct competition with Amazon S3. As we have explored cloud-based storage earlier, we shall not go into Rackspace Files further. Rackspace *Sites* is essentially a minimal PaaS service that runs PHP (and some other languages) and MySQL (and some other databases) on your behalf. The primary advantage for PHP developers is that it load-balances and scales automatically. This abstracts away a lot of the complexity required to manage elasticity. This is a good option if you're running a simple PHP setup that requires only run-of-the-mill PHP. However, if you run bleeding-edge libraries and PHP extensions, or want to take the details of scalability in your own hands then Rackspace Sites is not for you. You are at the peril of Rackspace with regards to the environment in which your PHP application runs. For example, Rackspace Sites still only had PHP 5.2 installed on 20th November 2009, more than four months after PHP 5.3 had been released. You are also not fully able to install and control supporting libraries and packages that are so essential for extending PHP.

Rackspace *Servers* finally provides complete control. It is in essence a virtualized server instance that we can log onto as root to do whatever we want (install libraries, upgrade PHP versions, etc.). So, we will look into utilizing the flexibility that Rackspace Servers provides to implement automated elasticity for PictureMe.

Distributed Processing for PictureMe

As we saw in Figure 4.5, the `_putColorGrid` method is a potential bottleneck. Even though Gmagick is relatively efficient, image processing is generally one of the rather resource-intensive tasks that a web application may do. The functions that relate to HTTP communication to Amazon too are rather time consuming relative to other functions that only require local execution. To prevent this bottleneck, we shall farm out these processes to individual workers (separate Rackspace Servers) using Gearman[16].

Gearman defines a set of worker and client APIs that are used along with a job server (Gearmand) that allocates work requests from clients to workers. Workers register themselves with the job server to work on jobs and clients create jobs and send them to the job server. See Figure 5.8 for how the color-grid processing for PictureMe will look with Gearman in place.

---
[16] http://gearman.org/

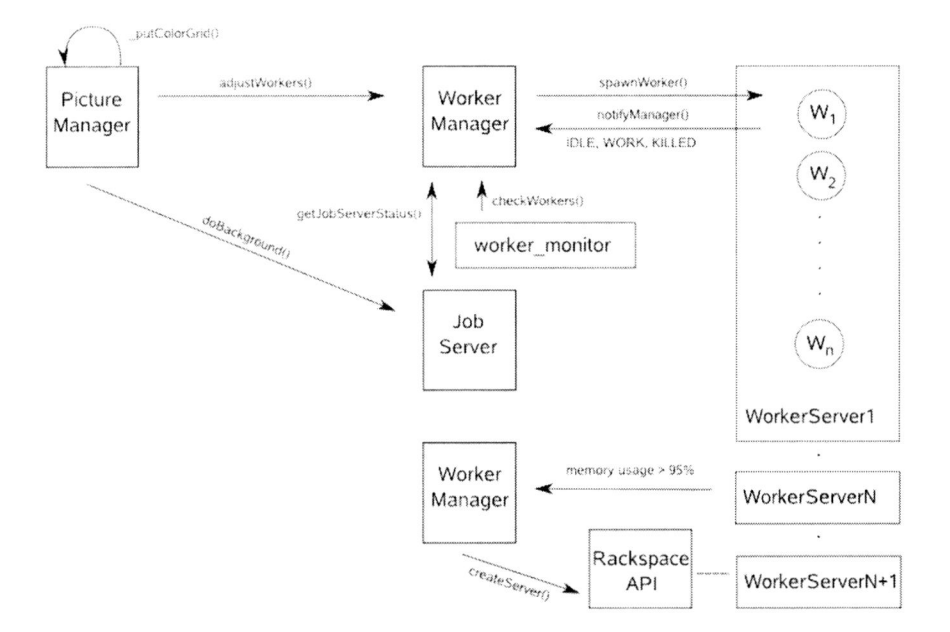

Figure 5.8

The Gearman APIs and job server can be obtained from the Gearman website[17] along with installation instructions (which we won't repeat here since it's fairly easy to install). To start the Gearman job server, do:

```
$ gearmand -d -u root
```

Now, let's go through each of the steps above in more detail.

Tackling the Bottleneck: _putColorGrid of PictureManager

If you look into the Gearman-enabled version of PictureMe, you'll find that PictureManager now delegates the heavy job of color-grid processing to a separate worker process, as shown below:

```
$this->_workerManager->adjustWorkers("putColorGridDelegated");
$jobStatus = $this->_gearmanClient->doBackground("putColorGridDelegated",
    $pictureName);
return ($this->_gearmanClient->returnCode() === GEARMAN_SUCCESS) ? TRUE : FALSE;
```

A call to adjustWorkers is first made on the _workerManager instance (which we'll look at in more detail soon). This ensures that there will be sufficient workers to do the `putColorGridDelegated` job. Then, we tell _gearmanClient to do the `putColorGridDelegated` job, informing the worker that picks up the job of the `$pictureName` (the worker will pick up the picture from cloud storage).

Gearman allows clients to create jobs that run in the background without having to wait for the completion of the job. This allows developers to let time-consuming jobs, such as color-grid creation in this case, run in the background while providing the end user with a quick response.

The `returnCode()` call on _gearmanClient just indicates if the task has been successfully sent to the job server. It does not indicate that the grid has been created. Since failure of color grid creation should not be a bother to the end user, he or she should not have to wait for a successful response from the task. In the case where color-grid creation is unsuccessful, the Gearman client can log this, and an application administrator can take action by regenerating the color-grid representation of

---

[17] http://www.gearman.org

the picture that is already available in the picture bucket. We will explore this when we look at the putColorGridDelegated worker.

WorkerManager

Central to the whole delegated grid-processing ecosystem is the _workerManager. The _workerManager monitors and manages worker servers and workers. Let's first take a look at how _workerManager ensures that there are always workers in abundance within the ecosystem to do _putColorGridDelegated jobs:

```
public function adjustWorkers($function)
{
   $status = $this->getJobServerStatus();
   if (($status["{$function}"]['in_queue'] > 0) || ($status["{$function}"]['
       capable_workers'] === 0)) {
      $this->spawnWorker();
   }
}
```

Upon a call to adjust the amount of workers in the ecosystem, _workerManager calls getJobServerStatus to find out the amount of jobs that are in a queue (meaning they are waiting to be processed), the number of jobs that are currently running and the amount of workers that are capable to run jobs:

```
public function getJobServerStatus()
{
   $response = $this->_jobServerCommand('status');
   $functionStatus = array();
   $functions = explode('\n', $response);
   foreach ($functions as $function) {
      if (!strlen($function)) {
         continue;
      }
      list($functionName, $inQueue, $jobsRunning, $capable) = explode('\t',
          $function);
      $functionStatus["{$functionName}"] = array(
         'in_queue' => $inQueue,
         'jobs_running' => $jobsRunning,
         'capable_workers' => $capable);
   }
   return $functionStatus;
```

```
    }
    protected function _jobServerCommand($command)
    {
        fwrite($this->_jobServer, "{$command}\r\n", strlen("{$command}\r\n"));
        $ret = '';
        while (true) {
            $data = fgets($this->_jobServer, 4096);
            if ($data == '.\n') {
                break;
            }
            $ret .= $data;
        }
        return $ret;
    }
```

At the time of writing, there are no functions or class methods within the Gearman PECL extension to issue the 'status' command to the Gearmand job server. What we do is open a socket connection to port 4730 and talk to it with the stream functions. We then iterate through the returned string to form the status array that we want. It's a bit of a hack, but it gives us access to more features available with the gearmand job server than the current PHP API provides.

Going back to `adjustWorkers`, the `_workerManager` will spawn a new worker if the job queue is not empty (when `adjustWorkers` is called) or if there are no capable workers for the `putColorGridDelegated` job.

Spawning Workers

The following code illustrates how we spawn new workers. We want to achieve scalability so you might think that we're going to create a new server instance at this point. However, one server instance can run multiple workers, so we're just going to assume that there is a server instance available that has capacity left. In a separate process that we will look at later we will take care of actually creating new server instances when the existing ones are getting overloaded.

```
    public function spawnWorker()
    {
        if ($this->_localStore->get('latestServerIndex') === NULL) {
            $latestServer = 'localhost';
            $serverPassword = WORKER_SERVER_PASSWORD;
```

```
        } else {
            $latestServerName = 'Worker'.$this->_localStore->get('latestServerIndex');
            $latestServerObject = unserialize($this->_localStore->get(
                $latestServerName));
            $latestServer = $latestServerObject->server->addresses->public[0];
            $serverPassword = $latestServerObject->server->adminPass;
        }
        $conn = ssh2_connect($latestServer, 22);
        if (!($conn) || !(ssh2_auth_password($conn, WORKER_SERVER_USERNAME,
            $serverPassword)) ||
        !($stream = ssh2_exec($conn, SPAWN_WORKER_COMMAND))
        ) {
            throw new Exception('Worker spawn failed.');
        }
    }
}
```

When `spawnWorker()` is called, `_workerManager` creates a worker on the latest server spawned. The index of the latest server spawned is obtained from the `_localStore`. If there is no recorded index for the latest server, the `_workerManager` will spawn a new worker on localhost. This is usually the case initially, when PictureMe has just started operations and memory resources are still available within the primary server where PictureMe is hosted. In the event where there is a separate server spawned, we use the index to obtain connectivity information to the latest spawned server.

We spawn a new worker by starting a process on the latest server using the SSH2 extension. This process is the worker that will register itself with the job server to do `putColorGridDelegated` jobs.

The Worker

Every time a new worker is started, the worker PHP script first generates a unique `$workerReference` for itself:

```
$workerReference = urlencode(time().getmypid());
```

This allows us to identify our worker, especially if we have a custom `_workerManager` that manages these workers. We use Unix time and process ID to create a unique identification reference for our worker. For those using PHP 5.3 and above, you may want to use `hostname().getmypid()` to add more information to this unique reference. Anyhow, process ID alone is unlikely to be unique enough to securely identify workers.

Next, we need to notify the _workerManager of the existence and identity of this newly spawned worker. The code below runs within our new worker.

```
notifyManager('idle');
function notifyManager($status, $reference = NULL)
{
   global $workerReference;
   if (is_null($reference)) {
      $reference = $workerReference;
   }
   $ch = curl_init(WORKER_SERVER_SERVICE.'?'.$status.'='.$reference);
   curl_setopt($ch, CURLOPT_HEADER, 0);
   curl_setopt($ch, CURLOPT_USERPWD, WORKER_SERVER_USERNAME.':'.
      WORKER_SERVER_PASSWORD);
   curl_exec($ch);
   curl_close($ch);
}
```

The worker communicates with the _workerManager by doing a cURL call to the worker server service on the primary server, indicating its status and identifying itself. The URL for this service is stored in WORKER_SERVER_SERVICE. We use Apache's built-in basic authentication mechanism[18] as a simple way to make sure that only workers with the given username and password can send notification signals to the _workerManager. There are more security considerations with regards to worker, job server and worker manager communication, and we shall discuss these subsequently.

Next, we start an instance of a GearmanWorker, register it with the job server and add two functions that that the worker can do. The first, putColorGridDelegated, is similar to the initial putColorGrid() within PictureManager. The worker obtains the picture from cloud storage with the given $pictureFile information and stores picture grids back into cloud storage. One notable addition that a worker does is the notification signals it sends to the _workerManager at the beginning of a job and upon completion. The _workerManager relies on these signals to monitor the activity of workers and determine their livelihood. The other thing that the delegated

---
[18]http://httpd.apache.org/docs/1.3/howto/auth.html#basic

putColorGrid() function does is that it notifies the _workerManager in the case of any error via notifyManager('error', $pictureFile).

```
$worker = new GearmanWorker();
$worker->addServer(JOB_SERVER_IP);
$worker->addFunction('putColorGridDelegated', 'putColorGrid');
$worker->addFunction($workerReference, "kamikaze");
while ($worker->work());
function kamikaze($job)
{
   notifyManager('killed');
   echo "hhaiiiiiyakk!";
   exit;
}
```

The other function that is registered is the kamikaze() function, which simply causes the worker process to stop. It is registered with the $workerReference on the job server so that the _workerManager can call this unique reference to stop an idling worker. It is a good practice to build in such 'scale down' capabilities, because unused servers in a cloud environment will cost us money.

Monitoring Workers

While Gearman dispatches jobs to an available worker, the _workerManager observes how many workers are running, whether these workers are busy and working optimally and kills off idle workers. It also starts new worker processes if a job queue is detected or if there are no workers that are able to perform the _putColorGridDelegated job. As an alternative to our proposed solution, the Gearman Monitor project[19] aims to do something similar, but development has not yet begun at the time of writing. In the meantime, we implement a simple service that listens to work/idle signals from workers that, coupled with the job queue status checking in adjustWorkers() that we have seen earlier and another timed process, allows us to achieve the level of monitoring and control that we want. Here is an excerpt of worker_server_service.php:

```
...
```

---

[19] https://launchpad.net/gearup

```php
    if (isset($_GET['idle'])) {
        $workerServerManager->workerStatus('IDLE', $_GET['idle']);
    } else if (isset($_GET['work'])) {
        $workerServerManager->workerStatus('WORK', $_GET['work']);
    } else if (isset($_GET['killed'])) {
        $workerServerManager->workerStatus('KILLED', $_GET['killed']);
    } else if (isset($_GET['error'])) {
        error_log('Message: Job Error. Time: '.time().'. File: '.$_GET['error']);
    }
}

public function workerStatus($status, $workerReference)
{
    $this->_localStore->put('WRK'.$workerReference, $status.'|'.time());
}
```

The statuses that workers submit are stored within `_localStore` with a WRK prefix to the worker reference. The time is stored as well so that the `_workerManager` can find out the duration for which a particular worker has been in its last status. Earlier we have looked at the conditions in which a new worker is spawned within `adjustWorkers()`, so let's take a look at how a worker is killed when it has been idling for too long. This is done within the worker_monitor.php process described below.

```php
$workerManager = WorkerManager::getInstance();
while(TRUE) {
    sleep(WORKER_MONITOR_FREQUENCY);
    try {
        echo "Checking workers...".PHP_EOL;
        $workerManager->checkWorkers();
    } catch (Exception $e) {
        error_log("Exception caught checking workers: ".$e->getMessage());
    }
}
```

worker_monitor.php is an ongoing process that calls `checkWorkers` at a preset `WORKER_MONITOR_FREQUENCY`. `checkWorkers()` on the other hand retrieves worker statuses from the `_localStore`, checks if a worker is idle, and kills the worker if it has been idling past a preset `IDLE_ALLOWANCE`. This final bit of worker management code is outlined below.

```
public function checkWorkers()
{
   $workers = $this->_localStore->get($this->_localStore->fwmKeys("WRK",
      WORKER_LIMITS));
   foreach ($workers as $workerName => $status) {
      list($activity, $since) = explode('|', $status);
      if (($activity === 'IDLE') && ((time() - $since) > IDLE_ALLOWANCE)) {
         $this->killWorker($workerName);
      } else if ($activity === 'KILLED') {
         $this->_localStore->out($workerName);
      }
   }
}
```

checkWorkers retrieves the statuses of workers from _localStore (a TokyoTyrant object) by using its fwmKeys() method. The fwmKeys(string $prefix, int $max_recs) method returns an array of key/value pairs that are prefixed with $prefix.

Monitoring Worker Servers

So far, we've been starting workers on the latest server instances that were created. We have not yet seen exactly how and when those server instances are created. To achieve automatic elasticity, we need to make sure that our application ecosystem grows and shrinks according to the resource requirements brought upon by usage. We want to preserve overall application performance to maintain user experience even when user volume grows tremendously. To do this, we need to make sure that all worker servers are performing optimally and are not taxed beyond their capability.

Performance analysis and monitoring is a vast subject itself. There are a few high-level factors such as memory, disks, CPU and network but almost all considerations will require an analysis of the resource requirement of the application (worker) that you are running and the environment in which the application resides. In our case, we are only monitoring and acting upon memory loads for the sake of example brevity.

We will use *monit*[20] as a memory usage monitoring mechanism. Whenever a server reaches 95% memory usage, we will spawn a new worker server. When mem-

---
[20] http://mmonit.com/monit/

ory usage falls below 30% (the memory usage of an Ubuntu Rackspace Server with 256MB), we will kill the worker server for cost efficiency. This is elasticity in action. The following is a configuration for the monit control file (monitrc) that does this partially:

```
check system localhost
    if memory usage > 95% then exec "/usr/bin/curl -u [USERNAME]:[PASSWORD] http
        ://[PRIMARY_SERVER]/pictureme/Distributed/worker_server_service.php?spawn
        =yes"
    if memory usage < 30% then exec "[PATH_TO_PICTUREME]/pictureme/Distributed/
        server_files/kamikaze.sh"
```

There are other possible test parameters such as `loadavg(TIME)`, `cpu usage(user)`, `cpu usage(system)` and `cpu usage (wait)`. This script is the same for all but the primary server that shouldn't shut itself down (otherwise there won't be any workers left!). This is easily done by removing the last line, so our primary server runs this script without this last kamikaze line. We have the above script in all worker servers spawned from the worker server image and run the primary worker server on the principal server in which the PictureMe application is hosted. Within `kamikaze.sh`, we get the hostname and pass it to the worker server service so that the `_workerManager` knows which server to stop.

Starting Up a New Worker Server

We use the *phprackcloud* library[21] to create a new server on Rackspace Servers. First, we obtain the latest server index and increment it by one. This server index is important to name the server for identification as we shall see very soon. We then call `createServer()` on the Rackspace service object passing in the `$workerName`, the `WORKER_SERVER_IMAGE_ID`, and 1 as the server flavor that we desire. A `stdClass` object containing a hierarchical representation of information on the newly created server will be returned by `createServer()`, which we will store within the `_localStore`. This object is useful whenever we need information such as the IP address, SSH password, etc. An example of a situation where such information is required is the spawning of workers that we have looked at earlier. We also store the latest server index in

---
[21] http://code.google.com/p/phprackcloud/

_localStore so that we can increment it for worker naming the next time a new server needs to be spawned. Below you'll see our spawnServer logic.

```php
public function spawnServer()
{
    $latestServerIndex = $this->_localStore->get('latestServerIndex') ? $this->
        _localStore->get('latestServerIndex') : 0;
    $latestServerIndex++;
    $workerName = 'Worker'.$latestServerIndex;
    $server = $this->_service->createServer($workerName, WORKER_SERVER_IMAGE_ID,
        1, NULL);
    if (is_null($server->cloudServersFault)) {
        $this->_localStore->put($workerName, serialize($server));
        $this->_localStore->put('latestServerIndex', $latestServerIndex);
    } else {
        throw new Exception('Unable to spawn new worker server.');
    }
}
```

Stopping a Worker Server

Of course we must not only create new servers when we need them; we should also stop servers if we no longer need them, to save resources. There are some considerations when stopping a server. We need to make sure that all workers on the server have completed the job that they are doing before shutting down the server. So, the first thing to do before killing a server is to stop gracefully all worker processes that are running on the server, allowing all workers to complete their job before killing itself. Again, we use fwmKeys() to retrieve worker keys, but this time we supply the $serverName as well to retrieve only worker names for a particular server. We only need the name of each worker to kill:

```php
public function killServer($serverName)
{
    if ($this->killAllServerWorkers($serverName)) {
        $server = unserialize($this->_localStore->get($serverName));
        $response = $this->_service->deleteServer($server->server->id, TRUE);
        if (!is_null($server->cloudServersFault)) {
            throw new Exception('Unable to kill worker server.');
        }
```

```
      }
   }
   public function killAllServerWorkers($serverName)
   {
      try {
         $workerNames = $this->_localStore->fwmKeys("WRK".$serverName,
            WORKER_LIMITS);
         foreach ($workerNames as $workerName) {
            $this->killWorker($workerName);
            while ($this->_localStore->get($workerName) !== 'KILLED');
            $this->_localStore->out($workerName);
         }
         return TRUE;
      } catch (Exception $e) {
         throw new Exception("Exception caught killing all workers");
      }
   }
```

After calling `killWorker()`, we wait for a signal from the worker indicating that it has been killed before removing its record from `_localStore`. It is necessary to wait for this signal as the worker might be busy doing another job and we want the worker to complete that job before killing itself. After all workers are killed, we call `deleteServer` on the Rackspace service, passing in the server's ID (obtained from the `$server` object stored when creating the server) and a confirmation. By waiting for the current jobs to finish, we don't have to move the existing jobs to the remaining servers (which would be very difficult).

The Worker Server Image

The `WorkerManager` class contains a method that you can call to create an image of a worker server that you can use to spawn new servers. On top of the other requirements required to run PictureMe mentioned in earlier chapters, these workers server will also need the following:

- Monit

- Gearman server, library and PHP extension

If you are interested in testing the concepts described in this section, the code to be placed on a worker server is available within the Distributed directory of the PictureMe application source. In any case, be sure to adjust some settings within the configuration files according to your setup.

Note: If your worker performs memory-intensive tasks, you might have to increase the memory limit that a PHP script is allowed to allocate by changing the `memory_limit` directive.

Authentication

We have gone through the process of creating an automatically elastic ecosystem using Rackspace Server's API and some very useful tools and extensions. In practice, there is a further need to limit access to the job server and the worker manager to prevent unauthorized clients, unauthorized workers and other forms of malicious interaction with the worker server service. For the worker server, we have implemented a basic HTTP authentication mechanism, but this may not be ideal in a production environment and it is recommended that something stronger is implemented. As for the job server, SASL/TLS secure authentication is planned and approved within Gearman's Launchpad blueprints ((See sasl-support and tls-support[22]). (Introduced at Launchpad[23], blueprints are a kind of lightweight specification of features that will or need to be worked on. Its main purpose is to help planning but bear in mind that it is by no means a guarantee that a particular feature will be available anytime soon). In the meantime, the best way is to allow only spawned worker access using `iptables` rules. For example, the following blocks all access to port 4730 except for access from `allowed_ip`:

```
#iptables -A INPUT -p tcp -s 0/0 --dport 4730 -j DROP
#iptables -A INPUT -p tcp -s [allowed_ip] --dport 4730 -j ACCEPT
```

The first line tells `iptables` to drop all traffic to port 4730 (Gearman's IANA (Internet Assigned Numbers Authority) registered port) while the second line makes an exception to this for [allowed_ip].

---

[22] https://blueprints.launchpad.net/gearmand
[23] https://launchpad.net/+tour/feature-tracking

Conclusion

What we have gone through with Rackspace and PictureMe elasticity is meant to provide you with a feel for how elasticity can be automated, and the various Rackspace server attributes and tools that can help in the process. The web services API provided by Rackspace and other cloud providers has made elasticity very much more convenient and relatively instantaneous. Gearman is a viable option to consider for such purposes and one of the friendliest ways to perform PHP-based message queuing.

Note that we could have easily used Amazon EC2 for this example, and you'll find that using it in such a scenario is remarkably similar. Since we have used Amazon's services already in the first parts of this chapter, and we want to show different cloud solutions as examples, we have built this part of the chapter using Rackspace Servers.

Microsoft's Azure Cloud

Microsoft's naming of its cloud-computing platform sure is strange. Azure is often associated with a blue that can be seen in the sky on a bright, clear day with no clouds in sight. Conspiracy theory aside, Azure is a cloud application platform that will be appealing to developers who are familiar with Microsoft technologies. In essence, the Azure platform is a group of technologies that provides access to Microsoft's cloud consisting of:

- Windows Azure
- SQL Azure
- AppFabric (formerly known as .NET services)

We'll be looking at these three services to see how we can use Microsoft's cloud in combination with PHP.

Windows Azure

Windows Azure is essentially a Windows operating-system instance that lives on Microsoft's cloud. Azure's cloud-based storage service is part of this offering, allowing the storage of BLOBs (binary large objects), message queues (to facilitate communication between components of Windows Azure applications) and even tables.

When starting up, Azure provides a browser-accessible portal[24] that allows you to create a hosting account for running applications, a storage account for storing data, or both. Developers can control the behavior of applications via a configuration file. This control file can, for example, be used to fix the number of instances of an application to run.

Each application instance can either have a web or worker role and runs on its own virtual machine (VM). A web instance accepts incoming HTTP (or HTTPS) requests via an IIS (Internet Information Services) running on the VM whereas a worker instance typically gets its input via a queue residing on Azure's storage. This concept of web and worker roles promotes separation of presentation layer from service layer. Also on the VM is a Windows Azure agent that serves as a point of interaction between the application and the overall Windows Azure fabric that governs all instances. The agent provides an API that allows applications to log events or send e-mail, IM or other messages to specified recipients via the fabric.

It is important to note that web instances have to be stateless to allow scalability as the load-balancer may not send requests from the same user to the same instance. User states have to be maintained somewhere else or implemented with the use of cookies.

As with most other cloud services, a REST/XML interface is available to access Windows Azure's functionalities, and a relatively comprehensive PHP wrapper[25] is available. Azure storage is covered by the Simple Cloud initiative as well. We can use Simple Cloud's Storage API to interact with Blob Storage, Queue API to interact with Queue Storage and Document API to interact with table storage.

The code sample we will be using to illustrate Azure usage includes a `CloudStorage` class (`CloudStorage.php`) that is interchangeable with the S3 class for use within the example PictureMe application. It implements an interface that is almost similar to the included S3 class, to make it easier to run the same example but this time using Microsoft's storage solution. We will also be using Zend's `SimpleCloud` abstraction layer to make it easier to talk to Azure.

---

[24] https://windows.azure.com/Cloud/
[25] http://phpazure.codeplex.com

98 ■ Working with Popular Cloud Infrastructures

To try out PictureMe and the `CloudStorage` class that actually uses Windows Azure's storage instead of Amazon's S3, sign up for an Azure account. Then, create a new service via your Azure portal, choosing 'Storage' as the type of service, and specify a service label and a public name associated with your storage endpoint. You will be given three endpoint URLs (Blob, Queue and Table) and a primary access key, among others.

We are interested in the Blob end-point. You will be able to obtain the account host and name that is used by Simple Cloud from the storage URL. Say if your endpoint URL is: `http://pictureme.blob.core.windows.net/`, then "pictureme" is your account name and `blob.core.windows.net` your host. Place this information within the `AZURE_*` constants in `config.inc.php`. These will subsequently be used within `constructAzureStorage()` of `CloudStorage` where we obtain the adapter for Azure storage:

```
$azureOptions = array(
    'storage_adapter'     => 'Zend_Cloud_Storage_Adapter_WindowsAzure',
    'storage_host'        => AZURE_STORAGE_HOST, //Endpoint
    'storage_accountname' => AZURE_ACCOUNT_NAME,
    'storage_accountkey'  => AZURE_ACCOUNT_KEY,
    'storage_container'   => 'pictureme'// Bucket
);
$this->_adapter = Zend_Cloud_Storage_Factory::getAdapter($azureOptions);
```

PictureMe shows images to the user by pointing the user directly to the image's location via the src attribute of an `<img>` tag without requiring any authentication at this point. Hence, we need to make the container that stores the images public so that it is accessible by the user. ACL is not yet implemented within the Windows Azure adapter in SimpleCloud at the time of writing, so we add the following line to the constructor to achieve this. This modification is commented in the version of Zend Framework distributed with the example, so you'll need to uncomment to follow this walk through.[26] Feel free to experiment with other visibility settings to suit your needs. The default ACL is `PRIVATE`.

```
$this->_storageClient->setContainerAcl($this->_container,
    Zend_Service_WindowsAzure_Storage_Blob::ACL_PUBLIC);
```

---

[26]See line 83 of `Zend/Cloud/Storage/Adapter/WindowsAzure.php`

Specify the public URL to the storage container at the STORAGE_RESOURCE_URL constant within config.inc.php. Usually, this URL takes the form of `http://[account_name].blob.core.windows.net/[container_name]`.

The last step is to define the `SIMPLECLOUD` constant in `config.inc.php` as Azure. PictureManager will then use a CloudStorage object for storage with Azure as the provider instead of an object of the S3 class as seen from the following snippet taken from PictureManager:

```
$this->_storage = SIMPLECLOUD ? new CloudStorage(SIMPLECLOUD) : new S3(
    ACCESS_KEY, SECRET_KEY, false);
```

Accessing the PictureMe application from the browser, you should be presented with a fresh PictureMe application that stores pictures onto Windows Azure's storage. Methods within `CloudStorage` mostly map to the underlying SimpleCloud implementation, customizing return values so that it is similar to S3's. Of interest is the specification of the 'returntype' option in `listItems()`:

```
$this->_adapter->listItems('', array('returntype' => 2)
```

If we were to just do `$this->_adapter->listItems(")`, we will only get an array of available images as strings of filenames. By specifying a returntype of 2, we get a list of objects, with each object containing a lot more details, for example:

```
[1] => Zend_Service_WindowsAzure_Storage_BlobInstance Object
(
    [_data:protected] => Array
        (
            [container] => pictureme
            [name] => 100px-Yakovsvetoslavcoin.jpg
            [etag] => 0x8CC6FF3A884149C
            [lastmodified] => Sat, 30 Jan 2010 18:46:24 GMT
            [url] => http://vito.blob.core.windows.net/pictureme/100px-
                Yakovsvetoslavcoin.jpg
            [size] => 3367
            [contenttype] => application/octet-stream
            [contentencoding] =>
            [contentlanguage] =>
            [isprefix] =>
            [metadata] => Array
```

```
            (
            )
        )
    )
```

These details do not just allow us to maintain a return value that is similar to S3's; but it is important for PictureManager as well as this information is used to sort and show pictures.

SQL Azure

Built on Microsoft SQL Server technologies, SQL Azure is ideal for those looking to migrate existing SQL Server provisions to the cloud to maintain database reliability and availability without having to manage physical constraints. It is easy to procure as well, as most parts of setting one up can be performed via the browser-accessible portal. You can even synchronize a locally installed SQL Server with a SQL Azure instance in the cloud easily. Those hosting applications within the Azure cloud and using SQL Azure can also request that both the application and database be hosted within the same data centre. As an alternative to conventional databases, the web-accessible nature of SQL Azure allows features such as geographic specificity and data sharing to be built more conveniently. We won't be using SQL Azure in our examples, but feel free to give it a try and experiment.

AppFabric (Formerly Known as .NET Services)

.NET Services are a form of PaaS and consist of specific services such as access control and a service bus. The Access Control service allows Azure-hosted applications to grant access to user identities that is created on user systems (such as a user's Active Directory service). This is achieved by defining some identity transformation rules via a browser-based portal or API.

The Service Bus service, on the other hand, helps applications that provide web services. The Service Bus itself acts as a kind of registry where you can add your web services (or endpoints as they are called within Azure). Your company will be given a URI whereby your web services can then be accessed with a little more specificity based on the naming hierarchy of your choice. This makes your web services discoverable from the Service Bus. For each endpoint registered, an application must open a connection to the Service Bus. This connection will be held open by the Service Bus and users of the endpoint will interact via this connection. This has a few advantages; it resolves issues that may arise with changing IPs in an environment where NAT is used and it is also more secure as well as there is no port exposure required on the firewall.

Chapter 6

Working with Popular Cloud Platforms

In the previous chapter, we looked at various Infrastructure as a Service solutions. In this chapter, we're going to look at a higher level of abstraction and look at Platform as a Service offerings, beginning with Google's. To refresh your memory, Platform as a Service goes further than Infrastructure as a Service; we no longer care about virtual machines but treat the whole platform as a single entity.

Google App Engine

Google's cloud-building know-how is a critical core competency that enables it to achieve the success it has in terms of end-user experience on market-leading SaaS. Their experience with applications that have massive amounts of users such as Search and Gmail means that Google like no other knows how to scale. Behind the speed and instant scalability that most end users take for granted, Google has built a stronghold of infrastructure and technology that developers can now tap into. With App Engine, developers deploy applications within a secure Sandbox that Google scales and load-balances automatically.

App Engine and PHP

Google's App Engine is a PaaS that, besides automatically scaling, also provides a number of services, some of which are related to other offerings in the Google ecosystem. These services form useful building blocks for a typical web application:

- Memcache
- URL Fetch (for HTTP and HTTPS requests)
- Mail
- XMPP (for instant messages)
- Images
- Google Accounts
- Task Queues

With regards to access to these services, App Engine currently only supports Python and Java. There are no PHP APIs available. PHP developers will have to call Java or Python classes to access these services on App Engine, which is less than ideal. So it makes little sense to host PHP applications on App Engine if your primary intention is to make use of the convenience provided by these services. On the contrary even: if your application is deployed on a traditional PHP environment, you can already use all of these services in one way or another. For example, Memcache is available in PHP via the memcached extension. PHP extensions such as Gmagick can perform manipulations that are much more sophisticated than those provided in the Images service. For those that involve Google-specific products, such as Accounts, there are available web-based APIs[1] that can be used with PHP.

So as PHP developers, why would we care about App Engine? Well, App Engine's services do provide very convenient abstractions that hide the tediousness of maintaining these services from developers. That, however, is not such great news for PHP developers though. While abstractions by themselves may not be fully ideal as we are not able to fully control the underlying implementation, the most glaring downside

---
[1] http://code.google.com/apis/accounts/

from a PHP developer's perspective is that PHP cannot be used within App Engine in a straightforward manner. PHP scripts will not run on App Engine as it is not a supported language. There are ways to get around this (albeit, not straightforward), as we shall see in the next section, but PHP developers should really evaluate if it is worth the trouble going through these workarounds to use these services that are not exclusive to App Engine after all. If eventually a PHP developer finds no appeal in these additional services, the critical basis for decision-making boils down to two factors:

- how well the PHP application will run on App Engine, and
- how important it is to you to utilize Google's scalability.

For the first factor, PHP developers should be wary that Quercus (one way of running some form of PHP on App Engine which we will look at in the next section) is not ideal for applications that use the bleeding-edge version of PHP and its extensions. You are advised to check the capability of Quercus very carefully to ensure that it is suitable for your needs (e.g. if heavy Java interfacing is required, for applications that use only a subset of PHP features or for PHP applications that have been tested to work on Quercus with sufficient future support).

As for the second, Google is not the only PaaS that provides automatic scalability. Rackspace Sites, for example, provides PHP support in earnest (albeit, not fully bleeding-edge as well: see our section on Rackspace in chapter 5). Cost-wise, it is good to note that the App Engine is free within a certain quota that is sufficient to start with, though PHP developers should consider the time cost that may be involved when dealing with an environment that does not run conventional C-based PHP. Furthermore, if the intent is to achieve huge traffic or usage volume, then App Engine becomes a variable-cost that has to be quantified and compared, like other PaaS or IaaS.

A Look at Quercus

Quercus is a reimplementation of the PHP interpreter, but written in Java. It is not the C implementation of PHP from `php.net` that we all know and love. At its current stage at the time of writing, it seems more like a lagging snapshot of PHP at a particular point in time. For example, the Quercus available in Resin 4.0.3 (released in January 2010 - Resin is a PHP/Java application server by Caucho, the company behind Quercus. Quercus is part of the Resin distribution[2] and lacks the features introduced in PHP 5.3, such as anonymous functions and namespaces introduced in July 2009. Because of its open-source nature, there are always improvements made to the PHP source that sometimes result in behavioral changes (with functions, classes, etc.). Lagging behind will confuse PHP developers and can cause application compatibility issues. A practical example of such an issue can be seen within a commented piece of code (the gethostname() function) later on in this chapter.

This brings us to the next point, that of community involvement. The PHP core and PECL community consist of a large band of code contributors from around the world. PHP is one of those rare open-source projects in which the community prevails over commercial concerns. In many cases, the open-source solutions (such as extensions) are better embraced over the proprietary ones and for good reasons. The open-source PHP community has built a solid reputation on being very helpful in fixing bugs, acting upon feedback and giving advice. The level of comfort provided by the entire community to a PHP developer may be hard to emulate. Furthermore, the cost of general support is free. Quercus has yet to show the kind of community-level presence as traditional PHP.

On the flip-side, however, Quercus makes it possible to use a whole set of Java libraries from PHP code. It can use Java concepts, such as quoting from the Caucho site, "JMS, EJB, SOA frameworks, Hibernate, and Spring". This is, again, no silver bullet though. There are other ways of getting to Java from within conventional PHP such as the open source PHP/Java Bridge[3], the Java Bridge from Zend Server[4] or through an intermediary layer such as Gearman.

Finally, perhaps the most significant purpose of Quercus is its ability to allow scripts written in PHP to run in Java application servers such as Glassfish, Resin and, of course, App Engine.

---

[2] http://www.caucho.com/projects/resin/
[3] http://php-java-bridge.sourceforge.net/pjb/
[4] http://www.zend.com/en/products/server/

Working with Popular Cloud Platforms ■ 107

We've given you enough warnings by now; if Quercus is suitable for your needs, and you want to use it to run PHP in Google App Engine, then follow along as we give you an example of how to get it up and running.

Getting PHP Apps Running in App Engine through Quercus

Until Google supports PHP as an official App Engine language, Quercus is the only way to run PHP apps on Google's super scaling infrastructure. That's what we'll be doing in this section.

Download and install Google App Engine SDK4.

Create a WAR directory structure

We start by creating a series of directories as per the WAR layout[5]. This is a standard layout for Java web applications that specifies where different types of files and directories should be placed within a WAR directory. Developers using Zend Framework's MVC will be familiar with the benefits of such separation. There is a template of this structure available with the accompanying source code along with a sample application (in the AccessSample directory) that shows how to access the Google Account services available in the App Engine.

Download and install Quercus

We'll need to download the latest Resin release[6]. We're interested in the GoogleQuercusServlet. What we need is only the `resin.jar` available in the lib directory, which we place within `AccessSample/war/WEB-INF/lib`.

Create a web application deployment descriptor

The web application deployment descriptor is a file that provides information about our application. The descriptor is a `Web.xml` file that we need to create. This file needs to be placed in the `war/WEB-INF` directory. It determines the servlet that should be called when requests are made to the web server. First, we'll need to declare the

---
[5] http://java.sun.com/j2ee/tutorial/1_3-fcs/doc/WCC3.html
[6] http://www.caucho.com/download/

servlets that will be used within the application. This is just a bit of boilerplate XML code, so just copy what we provide here:

```
<servlet>
    <servlet-name>Quercus Servlet</servlet-name>
    <servlet-class>com.caucho.quercus.servlet.GoogleQuercusServlet</servlet-class>
</servlet>
```

We then tell App Engine that we want to direct requests for PHP files to the Quercus Servlet:

```
<servlet-mapping>
    <servlet-name>Quercus Servlet</servlet-name>
    <url-pattern>*.php</url-pattern>
</servlet-mapping>
```

For everything else, we send the user to `index.html`:

```
<welcome-file-list>
    <welcome-file>index.html</welcome-file>
</welcome-file-list>
```

Configure App Engine

We also need to create another file, called `appengine-web.xml`, also residing within `war/WEB-INF` directory. App Engine checks the `appengine-web.xml` file for a series of configuration settings which we'll look at now. First, we'll need to specify the application ID:

```
<application>[APPLICATION_ID]</application>
```

This ID can be obtained from the Administration Console of your App Engine account. Next, we specify the version:

```
<version>[VERSION_ID]</version>
```

The version tag is more useful than it seems. With App Engine, you are allowed to access a particular version of your application using http://[VERSION_ID].latest.[APPLICATION_ID].appspot.com.

The next step is very important. To prevent our PHP files from being served in the form of raw source (we don't want anyone to directly browse the PHP source files), we'll need to specify the following:

```
<static-files>
    <exclude path="/**.php"/>
</static-files>
```

The two ** indicate that the exclusion applies to all directories within the path recursively. Static files are contents that are served directly to the user and do not change. Examples of such files are images, stylesheets or even JavaScript. App Engine serves these files via dedicated file servers and caches[7]. On the other hand, there are the resource files, which are accessible by the application via the filesystem. These files will be stored on the application servers along with the application. Other than JSP files, all files in the application directory are typed as both static and resource by default. To explicitly ensure that PHP files are treated as resource and therefore available to the application, we do:

```
<resource-files>
    <include path="/**.php"/>
</resource-files>
```

Calling Java classes

Quercus allows the use of Java classes with some special syntax. To highlight this feature, we will create a Java class that manages user access information by using the Google Accounts API provided by App Engine. The code we write for this is below (yes, a Java code snippet in a book for PHP developers: how cool is that?!):

```
package access;
import java.util.Map;
```

---
[7] http://code.google.com/appengine/docs/java/config/appconfig.html#Static_Files_and_Resource_Files

```java
import java.util.HashMap;
import com.google.appengine.api.users.UserServiceFactory;
import com.google.appengine.api.users.User;
import com.google.appengine.api.users.UserService;
public class AccessManager
{
   UserService userService;
   User user;
   public AccessManager()
   {
      this.userService = UserServiceFactory.getUserService();
      this.user        = userService.getCurrentUser();
   }
   public Map<String, String> getAccessInfo(String hostname)
   {
      Map<String, String> accessMap = new HashMap<String, String>();
      if (this.user == null) {
         accessMap.put("url", this.userService.createLoginURL(hostname));
         accessMap.put("display", "Login");
      } else {
         accessMap.put("url", this.userService.createLogoutURL(hostname));
         accessMap.put("display", "Logout");
      }
      return accessMap;
   }
}
```

Access Manager is a typical Java class. When compiling the class, we'll need to specify the classpath where the App Engine classes are located. These classes (noted as APP_ENGINE_API in the terminal command below) are packaged within a JAR file located in the lib/user directory of the Google App Engine SDK. The filename of the JAR file is something like appengine-api-1.0-sdk-1.3.5.jar. You'll need to copy this file to the war/WEB-INF/lib/ directory of your application. With all that done, do:

```
javac -classpath ../../war/WEB-INF/lib/[APP_ENGINE_API].jar AccessManager.java
```

We can now use this Java class in our PHP application. When the getAccessInfo() method of this class is called from PHP, Quercus will convert the returned HashMap to a PHP array. Within Quercus, we are now able to use this Java class as if it were a PHP class, the only difference being the special import syntax:

```
<?php
import access.AccessManager;
$messenger = new AccessManager();
$hostname  = $_SERVER['hostname'];
$access    = $messenger->getAccessInfo($hostname);
echo "<a href='{$access['url']}'>{$access['display']}</a>";
?>
```

The above snippet displays a link that allows the user to log on to the application via Google Account's sign-on service. It is located within `index.php` of the main `war/` directory. Notice we use `$_SERVER['hostname']` instead of the `gethostname()` function available in PHP 5.3. Why? Because the function is not available in Quercus, one of the issues we described earlier.

Creating a sandbox to simulate App Engine

At this point, we are able to test out the application locally with the App Engine SDK, which contains a simulator that allows us to test an application before we deploy it to App Engine. Start the app server with the following command:

```
./[APP_ENGINE_SDK]/bin/dev_appserver.sh AccessSample/war/
```

`APP_ENGINE_SDK` is the path to the Google App Engine SDK we downloaded in Step 1. You should be able to view the application on `http://localhost:8080/`.

Deploying on Google App Engine

Applications that have been tested to work in the development application server within the App Engine SDK can then be deployed on App Engine itself. Again the SDK provides a way to do that easily:

```
./[APP_ENGINE_SDK]/bin/appcfg.sh --enable_jar_splitting update ./AccessSample/
    war
```

Once the application has been deployed successfully, it will be accessible publicly via: `http://[APPLICATION_ID].appspot.com/`. That's it, we've successfully deployed a PHP application on App Engine!

Administration and Monitoring

Google App Engine excels in terms of the usability of its administration console. While scalability is automatic and developers should not have to worry too much about performance, the insights provided by the console help with cost analysis, reporting and debugging.

The level of information, of course, is not as fine-grained as with locally installed tools that have access to the underlying operating system, but when working with a PaaS it is definitely sufficient. Most of the services available within App Engine have a set of related daily statistics accessible on the Quota Details section. If this is insufficient, we can add additional log information by using the `java.util.logging.Logger` class in our PHP code and view it in the Logger section of the administration console. For team-development, App Engine allows you to invite additional developers and check their activities on the Developers and Admin Logs section respectively.

Overall, the App Engine has the potential to be a viable application platform for a significant set of applications, but currently it is very much less appealing to PHP developers because of the very fact that PHP is not supported natively. It is also, after all, a PaaS, and places some degrees of constraint on the developer (e.g. some Java APIs are not accessible). On the other hand, it is a safe, convenient and probably the most comprehensive platform to quickly utilize the Google cloud and enjoy the tremendous amount of effort that Google continues to invest into improving it.

Rackspace Cloud Sites

We mentioned Rackspace Cloud Sites when we discussed the Rackspace Cloud in Chapter 5. The Rackspace Cloud Servers product is an Infrastructure as a Service solution, but their Cloud Sites solution is a Platform as a Service, built largely on the same technology but offering seamless scaling without having to worry about virtualized images.

An application hosted on Cloud Sites does not know it's running on a cloud. The platform acts as a single server to your PHP application. This means no worries about firing up instances, but there are more benefits. Consider the following snippet of code:

```
$fp = fopen('data/employees.txt', 'r');
$employees = fread( $fp, filesize('data/employees.txt'));
fclose($fp);
```

In an infrastructure cloud, we need to worry about where we are reading the file from: Is the file the same on all instances? Are we on the right instance that has the right piece of data? On Cloud Sites, what happens is that under the hood all the filesystem access is transparently routed to Rackspace's Cloud Files storage architecture. This means that the file is stored on a scalable storage that scales as needed. We'll look at Cloud Files again when we look at storage services in the next chapter, but the interesting thing here is that we don't actually notice that Cloud Files is being used. We're reading and writing files as if we're on an ordinary, single box. This makes development easier since you can add new developers to your team who have no clue about cloud computing and who can still write apps that run on Cloud Sites.

Another feature of Rackspace Cloud Sites is operating system abstraction. If we run a regular PHP file, our file is run on the Linux operating system. If the same application would contain a Microsoft ASP.net file, that file would be served on Windows. The platform automatically chooses the right operating system. If you had to compare this to a traditional single server solution, it would be like rebooting into another operating system on the fly whenever someone requests a file that should be opened by a different operating system. In this case, of course, there is no rebooting; the process is seamless. This is useful if we want to build PHP applications that interact with Microsoft technologies. We could run those on Windows while we're running our PHP on Linux within the same application.

There are a few limitations in Rackspace Cloud Sites; at the time of writing they only support PHP 5.2 even though 5.3 has been out for months, and there is no shell access nor an API. This means that you need to fall back on traditional deployment methods such as FTP or web dashboard access to get an application on the platform. The lack of an API means that it's not currently possible to "talk to the cloud" as we did with App Engine.

Another disadvantage might be the pricing. Pricing starts at $149 USD per month; although this gives you all the benefits of a scaling platform, it's still quite a bit more expensive than running a bunch of Virtual Private Servers or cloud instances on other platforms. Rackspace is renowned for their reliability and support, however, so if you're looking for a stable, solid platform solution, it's worth a look.

More information on Rackspace Cloud Sites can be found on the Rackspace homepage[8].

Other Platforms

There are a number of other vendors offering Platform as a Service solutions that support PHP. If you search the web for `platform as a service php` you'll find a number of vendors offering solutions. We must state, however, that there are not nearly enough solid platforms for PHP yet. Sure there are some, but Rackspace and Google aside, most of what you'll find out there are smaller, relatively unknown vendors. There is nothing wrong with smaller unknown vendors–on the contrary; but it is an indication that it's a market that hasn't fully matured yet. Infrastructure as a Service is represented by all the major vendors you can think of.

Maybe the PHP world isn't ready yet for Platform as a Service; maybe we're all still thinking too much in terms of "servers" and "clustering". Maybe we feel that we want to be in control of how the platform scales. Regardless of the reasoning behind it, in the coming years we'll probably see Infrastructure as a Service gaining more popularity before Platform as a Service solutions really catch on.

Or maybe someone just has to start the killer App Engine equivalent for PHP. If there's an entrepreneurial mind among our readers, take note: we believe there's opportunity to build something great.

---

[8] http://www.rackspacecloud.com/cloud_hosting_products/sites

Chapter 7

Working with Popular Cloud Software and Services

In this final chapter, we're going to look at how to use the third service model with PHP: software as a service. We're going to look at a number of service offerings and show you how to use those from within PHP applications.

Identification Using OpenID

Software as a Service gives us the ability to reuse components in the cloud, which works similar to reusing components or objects within an Object Oriented application, but at a different scale. Cloud applications should ideally reuse focused services within the public cloud as much as possible and focus on their own core business, as long as the use of these services does not introduce undesired security or performance risks. Identification services such as OpenID are an ideal candidate for reuse. Besides being able to provide a better user experience, developers are able to 'outsource' tedious chores such as sensitive password storage and management to a focused provider on the cloud. Users of the application benefit as well as they are able to conveniently log in without having to keep track of many different accounts and passwords. The fact that passwords are not stored within the application also serves well to enhance the feeling of confidence as there will be one less point of possible breach of password. This is important in a situation where the user has a common password for all or most of her activities.

OpenID is becoming increasingly prevalent, with a substantial number of influential identity providers on board (Google, Yahoo, Launchpad) and a lot of useful sites supporting OpenID as a way to log in (e.g. StackOverflow, LiveJournal). The identity provider, end-user and service provider all play a role within the OpenID identification ecosystem, as illustrated in Figure 7.1.

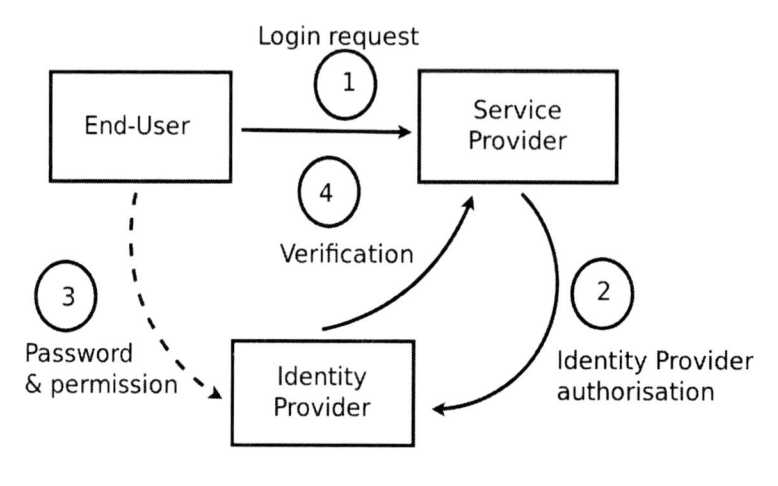

Figure 7.1

Figure 7.1 illustrates the relationship between the various actors within an OpenID identification ecosystem where the arrows represent transfers of responsibilities. There are other actors involved such as the user-agent (User-Agent is OpenID's terminology for the end user's web browser) which we omit to create a more high-level overview. We will walk-through the OpenID authentication process from the perspective of a UserManager object, used to add identification functionalities to our sample PictureMe application. We will be using the Zend_OpenId component of Zend Framework to handle the details involved. There are other libraries available as well, but Zend Framework's implementation seems to be the most up-to-date. Because in this case we don't want to add the whole of Zend Framework to our application but just the Zend_OpenId component, we need to add a constant to our config so the source doesn't depend on Zend_Session. This constant is named SID and must be set to true (If you're interested in finding out how `Zend_OpenId_Consumer` manages the presence of a `SID` constant, check out the `verify()` method of the `Zend_OpenId_Consumer` source code[1]. Hence, for PictureMe, we have this constant set to true in `config.inc.php` to avoid depending on `Zend_Session`. You will find in the PictureMe example source a stripped version of Zend Framework with only the `Zend_OpenId` components and some other supporting dependencies.

Login Request

The authentication process starts with the provisioning of an OpenID identifier from the end-user. An OpenID identifier is in the form of a unique URL. Those that wish to use an e-mail as an OpenID can use a translation service that conforms to the EAUT (Email Address to URL Translation protocol[2] such as emailtoid.net. Emailtoid.net helps turn e-mail addresses into fully qualified OpenID URLs. The request to log in is usually submitted via a form provided by the PHP application. PictureMe's OpenID login form is shown in Figure 7.2.

Figure 7.2

The identifier submitted by the user is passed on to a user agent, which PictureMe manages:

```
public function userLogin($openIdUrl)
{
   $this->_constructConsumer();
   if (!($this->allowedUser($openIdUrl) && $this->_consumer->login($openIdUrl, '
      access.php'))) {
      return false;
   }
}
```

---

[1] http://www.zendframework.com/code/
[2] http://eaut.org/

We'll first need an instance of `Zend_OpenId_Consumer`. This object contains methods that helps in the process of authenticating a user, details of which we shall see very soon. The first thing we do in the code above is to call `__constructConsumer()` which instantiates such an object if it isn't already instantiated. We do not instantiate `$this->_consumer` within the constructor as the UserManager object may have other responsibilities that do not require a `Zend_OpenId_Consumer` object all the time. `$this->allowedUser()` then checks if the user is allowed to use the application in the first place to save the trouble of going through the entire OpenID authentication process if the user is not allowed to use the software. The example source included with this book implements `allowedUser()` using a simple check with a file that lists the allowed users. A full implementation will probably involve a more complex user database.

Once the `allowedUser()` check passes, the UserManager calls the `login()` method on the `Zend_OpenId_Consumer` object, passing in the `$openIdUrl` and the URL of a verification handler which we will look at subsequently. The `login()` method encapsulates several steps in the authentication process. It first performs identifier normalization, which is essentially making sure that an OpenID URL conforms to the format as defined by the OpenID specification4. Then, it performs discovery where the claimed ID, provider URL and the OpenID protocol version is obtained. The Claimed ID is obtained after the normalization step we see earlier. This is the identifier that the end-user claims to own (the aim of the whole process is to verify this claim). Next, the `login()` method also secures. Subsequently, the login method sends an authentication request to the provider which brings us to the next step.

Identity Provider Authorization

The authentication request brings the end-user to the OpenID identity provider page where the end-user will be asked if she wishes to sign-in to an application with the OpenID that is hosted on the identity provider. If the end-user has not yet logged in to the identity provider, she will be asked to do so. Usually, the URL of the application that is to be accessed and the information that will be sent to the application will be displayed. Figure 7.3 is an example of such a sign-in page.

The end-user should confirm the sign in if she trusts the application and is willing to have the stated information sent to the application.

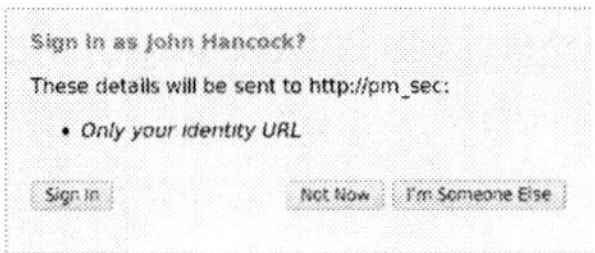

Figure 7.3

Verification

Once all authorization steps are completed on the identity provider, the process gets redirected to access.php along with some information that allows the Zend_OpenId_Consumer object to check that the authorization is valid. Here is an example of such validation:

```
public function verifyOpenId($params)
{
   $this->_constructConsumer();
   if ($this->_consumer->verify($params, $id)) {
      $this->setCurrentUser($id);
      return TRUE;
   } else {
      return FALSE;
   }
}
```

The $params passed to verifyOpenId() is simply an array of all HTTP request variables obtained from the $_REQUEST (which may contain some other cookie information that will be ignored) or $_GET superglobals. The verify() method takes these parameters and should check if the response is properly signed by the identity provider and subsequently assigns the OpenID to the $id variable. setCurrentUser() then starts a session and stores the $id in the session, allowing the end-user to access the application.

Thus far, we have implemented a mechanism to identify an end-user and to make sure the identity is a valid one by checking with the identity provider. We allow identified end-users that are allowed to access the application to log in and use PictureMe. We keep this list of allowed users in a text file for the purpose of example. We also reject users attempting to log in with an OpenID that is not in our allowed list.

We also provide no means of registering and to automatically add an OpenID to the allowed list. Some, more public, applications will want to allow end-users to register with the application if the OpenID provided is not in their database instead of rejecting the end-user's access. OpenID helps in this case as well in the form of the OpenID Simple Registration Extension protocol. The protocol allows OpenID enabled sites to obtain more detailed information from an end-user's profile (i.e. nickname, email, date of birth, gender, postcode, country, language and time zone). End-users will not need to enter this information again as an application can extract this information from the identity provider with the end-user's OpenID. This protocol is nicely wrapped within `Zend_OpenId`' as well within the `Zend_OpenId_Extension_Sreg` class. Using this you can effectively provision your application by creating a user on the fly based on the information that the OpenID provider gives you.

Authorization Using OAuth

In this section, we'll look at the OAuth authorization protocol. While OpenID allows developers to identify a user and to make sure that the identity is a valid one by checking with an identity provider, OAuth is different in the sense that it goes a step further and allows developers to access a user's protected data that is hosted on an OAuth-enabled service provider. Hence, OAuth is an important protocol in a developer's arsenal to build truly cloud-oriented applications that can access specialized resource data stores and services in a secure manner. Many market-leading web establishments have opened up access to their core services via OAuth since this standard has been established. Some of the more popular ones are Twitter, Digg, Flickr, Google and Yahoo. A good example of practical use of OAuth is the ability to use someone's Flickr photo's in a completely different application. Using OAuth, this application asks the user for permission to access their Flickr data, and Flickr will then provide the images to the application, without the user having to give his Flickr password to the third party application, which makes it quite secure.

OAuth is service-provider specific. Hence, you'll need to obtain the user's login handle to the target service provider to use any of the user-specific APIs. For convenience, some applications allow OpenID to be conveniently tied together with OAuth, in which case you don't have to worry what the user's ID is in various applications.

Let's have a go at accessing users' Google data via OAuth by extending the capability of PictureMe to include the display of the latest image uploaded to the user's Picasa account. PictureMe will display the latest image uploaded even if it is a private image which requires a sign-on to view. This is possible because the application will obtain authorization via OAuth.

Registering with the Service Provider

First we need to register PictureMe as an OAuth consuming application with the service provider; Google in this case. You can use Google's registration page[3] to access their user-specific services via OAuth. Registration enhances security and consequently, user confidence with your web application. It allows Google to know that it is in fact interacting with a known (registered) site when exchanging tokens.

For security, OAuth requests need to be signed with a digital signature so the provider can make sure the requests are coming from a valid source. One way of doing this is by uploading an X.509 cert at the URL we just mentioned. We will however use the HMAC-SHA1 signature method to sign requests as we shall see subsequently to avoid the need to upload a certificate file upon registration. Instead, place the OAuth consumer key and secret provided by Google into the PictureMe config file if you want to try out the example OAuth access within PictureMe.

Getting a Request Token

The OAuth PECL extension[4] is a fast package that can be used to perform most of the tasks required to access services that require OAuth authorization. As usual with PHP, there are alternatives as well but the extension is fast and straightforward. Most of the functionalities are encapsulated within an OAuth class. We instantiate an OAuth object as shown below:

```
$this->_oauth = new Oauth(OAUTH_CONSUMER_KEY, OAUTH_CONSUMER_SECRET,
    OAUTH_SIG_METHOD_HMACSHA1);
```

---

[3] https://www.google.com/accounts/ManageDomains
[4] http://pecl.php.net/package/oauth

The OAUTH_SIG_METHOD_HMACSHA1 constant passed into the method indicates that we intend to use HMAC-SHA1 as the signature method as per our intention when signing up.

We first need to obtain a request token from Google. For all cases in general, the request token serves as a basis for user authorization essential before an access token is given to a web application. In Google's case, the token also identifies the service which your application intends to access. This information is passed in the form of URLs specified within the scope parameter separated by a space. The URLs for each of Google's services, like Picasa[5] can be obtained within the documentation for the respective APIs. This URL should be placed within the scope parameter. The scope parameter identifies which Google service our application will need to access. For the range of available scopes, see the Google Data APIs Frequently Asked Questions[6] page. There is no method within the OAuth class to explicitly set the scope as it is a parameter that is unique to Google, so we pass it in the URL:

```
$scope = urlencode("http://picasaweb.google.com/data/");
$requestToken = $this->_oauth->getRequestToken("https://www.google.com/accounts"
    . "/OAuthGetRequestToken?scope={$scope}");
```

The getRequestToken() method returns an array of token information (the token itself, and the token secret) upon success. We then continue with the following code, where we store the token in our local storage.

```
$callback = urlencode("http://".$_SERVER['HTTP_HOST'].$_SERVER['PHP_SELF']);

$this->_localStore->put($_SESSION['userId'], serialize($requestToken));

header("Location: https://www.google.com/accounts/OAuthAuthorizeToken?
    oauth_token={$requestToken['oauth_token']}&oauth_callback={$callback}");
```

We store the token information in the _localStore with the user's ID as key. We will need this information later on to create the access token once the user has provided authorization to this request token. We are using TokyoTyrant here to persist this information, other storage can be used as well dependent on the desired level of so-

---

[5] http://picasaweb.google.com/data/
[6] http://code.google.com/apis/picasaweb/faq_gdata.html#AuthScopes

phistication and security. Finally, we redirect the user's browser to the authorization page at Google, passing the `oauth_token` and an `oauth_callback` so that the user gets redirected back to the application once she has confirmed authorization. We will look at how the application handles the OAuth process upon callback subsequently.

Getting an Access Token

Once the user has granted consent, Google passes the authorized token back to a defined `oauth_callback`. Much of what is performed in this callback is encapsulated in the `userAuthorized()` function, which is given the authorized `$token` as a parameter. The code below contains our implementation of `userAuthorized`.

```
public function userAuthorized($token)
{
   $userTokens = unserialize($this->_localStore->get($_SESSION['userId']));
   if ($token === $userTokens['oauth_token'] && !$this->getStoredAccessToken())
      {
      $this->_constructOAuth();
         $this->_OAuth->setToken($userTokens['oauth_token'],$userTokens["
            oauth_token_secret"]);
      $accessToken = $this->_OAuth->getAccessToken('https://www.google.com/
         accounts/OAuthGetAccessToken');
      $userTokens['access_token'] = $accessToken['oauth_token'];
      $userTokens['access_token_secret'] = $accessToken['oauth_token_secret'];
      $this->_localStore->put($_SESSION['userId'], serialize($userTokens));
   }
   return $this;
}
```

We first use the user's ID, which is still in our session after getting redirect back from Google, to retrieve the initial token. We then make sure that the token is valid for the user and that there is no access token stored. We associate the authorized request token that we retrieved from `_localStore` to the `$_OAuth` object by calling `setToken()`. We use this token as an exchange for an access token by calling `getAccessToken()`, passing in the `OAuthGetAccessToken` URL defined by Google. We then place the access token into `_localStore`. We will use this access token to interact with user resources and services via the appropriate API.

Fetching Resources

The OAuth fetch() method allows us to obtain OAuth protected resources and use services that are defined within an API. The Developer's Guide for the Picasa API[7] is available on the Google website.

The API will indicate the URL to use and any additional parameters required. To fetch information on the latest picture uploaded to Picasa, we write:

```
public function getLatestPicasaPicture($username)
{
    $access = Manager::getInstance('UserManager')->checkAuthorization()->
        getAccess();
    if ($access->fetch("http://picasaweb.google.com/data/feed/api/user/{$username
        }?alt=json&kind=photo&max-results=1")) {
        return json_decode($access->getLastResponse());
    } else {
        throw new Exception("Problem fetching from Picasa");
    }
}
```

The variable $access is an OAuth object with an access token from _localStore associated to it using setToken(). We use alt=json to obtain a JSON response, which is in turn decoded into an array via json_decode before being returned to the front-end.

The book's sample source code contains a working example of the use of OAuth as described. To try out the sample application, you will have to supply your own OAUTH_CONSUMER_KEY' and OAUTH_CONSUMER_SECRET in config.inc.php.

OAuth is definitely an innovative and important development which is increasingly becoming more popular, especially because SaaS services are becoming more prevalent. Specific access control for resources or services has always been one of the defining features of traditional enterprise applications. OAuth's introduction brings this kind of granularity to web services elegantly without the use of cumbersome passwords and compromise of security that password dissemination implies. It is also great that it is emerging as a popular standard used within the cloud over older or site-specific protocols.

---
[7]http://code.google.com/apis/picasaweb/docs/2.0/developers_guide.html

Search

Google Search

When it comes to search, the undisputed leader is Google, even within the search SaaS arena. Google's cloud started out as a way to handle the massive computational requirements and the enormous storage involved in its indexing process. Today, this cloud handles 9.3 billion core searches per month according to figures for May 2009 by ComScore[8].

Google's search results are appealing because of their ranking quality. Search users are often comfortable with the degree of relevance of the search results returned; confident that those appearing within the first few (highest ranked) results will be useful to the user. The degree of abstraction provided by Google's SaaS search offering is enormous. Not only does Google's search abstract away the need to configure the tons of servers required to crawl and index the web, there are many layers of software intelligence that go into ranking results whenever a search is requested. To produce those high quality rankings, there is of course the infamous PageRank algorithm. Other features are involved as well in the handling of language nuances, time suitability and personalization. Despite all the heavy-lifting that goes on behind the scenes when producing good search results, all we need from a PHP perspective is a simple cURL call to the Google AJAX Search API to add Google search as a SaaS component to our own application. Here is how to do this:

```
$searchString = rawurlencode('The Count of Monte Cristo');
$key         = ''; //Optional
$userIp      = ''; //Optional

$url  = "http://ajax.googleapis.com/ajax/services/search/web?v=1.0&q={
    $searchString}";
$url .= !empty($key) ? "&key={$key}" : '';
$url .= !empty($key) ? "&userip={$userIp}" : '';

$ch = curl_init();
curl_setopt($ch, CURLOPT_URL, $url);
curl_setopt($ch, CURLOPT_RETURNTRANSFER, 1);
$json_result = curl_exec($ch);
curl_close($ch);
```

---

[8] http://www.comscore.com/

```
$result = json_decode($json_result);
```

In the snippet above, we perform a GET via cURL, specifying a `$searchString` to obtain a set of search results that is JSON encoded. Decoding the result with PHP's `json_decode()` function, we get a `$result` object, which contains a `$result->responseData` object. This object further contains a `$result->responseData->results` array, which is an array of 4 result objects by default, each object having the following information:

```
stdClass Object
(
   [GsearchResultClass] => GwebSearch
   [unescapedUrl] => http://en.wikipedia.org/wiki/The_Count_of_Monte_Cristo
   [url] => http://en.wikipedia.org/wiki/The_Count_of_Monte_Cristo
   [visibleUrl] => en.wikipedia.org
   [cacheUrl] => http://www.google.com/search?q=cache:_guWtTloin8J:en.wikipedia.
      org
   [title] => The Count of Monte Cristo - Wikipedia, the free encyclopedia
   [titleNoFormatting] => The Count of Monte Cristo - Wikipedia, the free
      encyclopedia
   [content] => The Count of Monte Cristo (French: Le Comte de Monte-Cristo) is
      an adventure novel ...
)
```

Besides these objects, `$result->responseData` also contains a `$result->responseData->cursor` object, in which we can obtain the estimated total number of results via the `$result->responseData->cursor->estimatedResultCount` attribute. The `$result->responseData->cursor` object also contains an array of pages that allow you to obtain more results:

```
stdClass Object
(
   [pages] => Array
   (
      [0] => stdClass Object
      (
         [start] => 0
         [label] => 1
      )
```

```
[1] => stdClass Object
(
    [start] => 4
    [label] => 2
)
[2] => stdClass Object
(
    [start] => 8
    [label] => 3
)
...
```

To get more results, specify the start index detailed in the cursor object within the GET URL. For example, to get the set of result labeled with page 2, the following URL is required:

```
$url = "http://ajax.googleapis.com/ajax/services/search/web?v=1.0&&q={
    $searchString}&start=4";
```

The number of results returned can also be adjusted by specifying the rsz parameter in the URL:

```
$url= "http://ajax.googleapis.com/ajax/services/search/web?v=1.0&&q={
    $searchString}&rsz=large";
```

Optionally, a $key[9] can be specified so that Google knows who to contact in the event of any problem performing searches. You can obtain a key[10] for your site on the Google site. You'll need to provide the URL of your application, where the search request is from. A single key can only be used within a single directory (but does include sub-directories of that directory).

There are other customizable options such as type of search (Web, Video, Books, etc.), safe search filtering and country specificity, among others. For a comprehensive look at the API, check out Google's own reference documentation[11].

---

[9] http://code.google.com/apis/ajaxsearch/key.html
[10] http://code.google.com/apis/ajaxsearch/signup.html
[11] http://code.google.com/apis/ajaxsearch/documentation/reference.html

Twitter Search

One of the considerations of Google's ranking mechanism is the compatibility of the age of a page with the nature of the query. For example, a query such as "London weather" is best answered with the most current page whereas "London weather December 1895" (the year The Time Machine was published) should yield something more factual that has stood the test of time.

Real-time searches have become increasingly popular; users of the internet now use search to ease many aspects of their daily lives (check ticket availability, in-season groceries, weather, congestion, etc.) as opposed to searching for encyclopedic, knowledge-based information alone. There are often specialized sites that provide such real-time information, but the advent of social media such as Twitter now provides developers with the avenue to approach the retrieval of such information from a whole new perspective.

The winter of 2009/2010 in United Kingdom was the coldest since 1963. Heavy snowfall occurred around the few days leading up to Christmas and many days after, causing severe delays and stoppages on almost all modes of transport. Coincidentally, it was the time of the year where long distance road, air and rail Christmas travel around the UK and Europe is common. The result is utter pandemonium leading to many a tumultuous journey. But amidst all the chaos, a different source of information was emerging on the Twitter cloud, where people started to use the #uksnow tag when they had information relevant to the weather situation. All over UK and Europe, many were tweeting information about the snow. So, to find out what's happening with the snowy condition in the UK, one can search Twitter using the #uksnow tag yielding information on where snow was falling (with postcode level precision), what it looked like (with twitpic images), what it felt like and the fun or trouble it had caused. The cool thing about it is not just the timeliness of the information but also how easy it is to setup very meaningful real-time information structures. This power can be tapped in our applications, which is the next example we're going to look at.

Twitter can be searched via the exposed Search API in pretty much the same way as most REST-ful APIs. Similar to searching on Google, we use PHP's cURL functions to GET our desired $result, as shown:

```
$searchString = urlencode('#catan');
```

```
$format = 'json'; // json or atom
$url = "http://search.twitter.com/search.{$format}?q={$searchString}";
$ch = curl_init();
curl_setopt($ch, CURLOPT_URL, $url);
curl_setopt($ch, CURLOPT_RETURNTRANSFER, 1);
$json_result = curl_exec($ch);
curl_close($ch);
$result = json_decode($json_result);
```

After executing this code, $result contains an array of tweets in the form of:

```
stdClass Object
(
    [profile_image_url] => http://a1.twimg.com/profile_images/131711392/
        vito_normal.jpg
    [created_at] => Mon, 22 Feb 2010 17:57:48 +0000
    [from_user] => vitoc
    [to_user_id] =>
    [text] => More #catan with the BBC guys tonight! Continuing my more roads and
        settlements (vs. cities) policy.
    [id] => 9486011318
    [from_user_id] => 1478589
    [geo] =>
    [iso_language_code] => en
    [source] => <a href="http://twitter.com/">web</a>
)
```

Twitter Search requests need not be authenticated but do make sure that the search string is url-encoded. We use PHP's `urlencode()` function to do this in the snippet above. Twitter currently imposes a limit on the amount of API calls that can be made within an hour[12] but the threshold is not very constraining. Within a search string, operators such as hashtags (#) and attitude (e.g. :)) can be used to make searches more refined. See the Twitter documentation[13] for a complete list of possible operators. There are a number of optional parameters that can be specified as well, such as language (lang), locale, number of tweets to return per page (rpp) and the page to return. See the Twitter API documentation[14] for a complete list of possible parameters).

---

[12] http://apiwiki.twitter.com/Rate-limiting
[13] http://search.twitter.com/operators
[14] http://apiwiki.twitter.com/Twitter-API-Documentation

Operators and parameters are very important when using Twitter searches due to the social aspect and real-time nature of tweets and the usefulness of searches made on them. The Search API itself is a powerful tool for developers looking to build interesting applications that cover domains such as sentiment-analysis, crowd sourcing and social-graphing.

Payments

Google Checkout

Google Checkout is a payment service that lives in the cloud and is offered as a Software as a Service component to applications that need to process payments. It is a convenient way for buyers to make payments for purchases made at sites that support it. Typically, buyers will only have to click on the Google Checkout button on a site to buy items. If the buyer has a Google Checkout account, all she has to do is confirm the purchase. The cumbersome task of having to enter payment and delivery details on multiple sites is avoided.

Sites that support Google Checkout also benefit from the outsourcing of payment collection to the Google Checkout cloud. Besides making the purchasing process more convenient, buyers will be more inclined to purchase if they are comfortable that the payment is processed by a well-recognized entity, even more so if they had made successful past purchases easily and securely. On the security front, sellers can save a lot of time checking for possible fraud with Google Checkout's built-in fraud prevention filter. The associated cost for payment processing is also relatively cheaper for smaller-sized merchants as there are no charges for setting up a Google Checkout merchant account unlike many other payment solutions who often require a monthly fee. The range of cards supported by Checkout is not comprehensive but usually sufficient (Visa, Visa Electron, MasterCard, Maestro and Solo). Other features of Checkout include tax charges management, delivery charges handling, and Google analytics integration.

Integration with Google Checkout is very simple. It's not necessary to integrate much code or whole pages as with many other payment providers. Google Checkout integrates itself nicely in your own existing HTML code. So integration can be as easy as adding a simple HTML "Buy Now" button to your site. It is also simple to use Checkout's standard shopping-cart, again very tightly integrated into your own code. To do so, a snippet of JavaScript[15] with the appropriate Merchant ID is required before the <body> tag followed by some CSS annotations to product listings and descriptions on the selling pages. The CSS annotation consists of class assignments to HTML elements that contain product information. For example, a <div> of a product will have to be assigned the "product" CSS class. Child elements of the <div> will then contain further details with CSS classes such as product-image, product-title, product-shipping, product-attr-size and product-price. Be sure to match these classes with an appropriate element type (not all HTML elements can be recognized by Google Checkout). The Checkout Developers documentation[16] contains a comprehensive list of CSS classes that can be used to provide product information. Of importance also is the googlecart-add-button or googlecart-add CSS class that identifies the button (or another HTML element) that the shopping-cart JavaScript snippet will listen to. It should be a breeze to create these CSS class associations within the view of a properly structured, object-oriented PHP web application.

When a buyer clicks on the Google Checkout button, she gets redirected to a Google Checkout page that will list all the items that are in her shopping cart. Once she confirms her purchases, the seller will be notified. Subsequently the seller needs to actually trigger the charging of the buyer's card if Auto Charge is not enabled. The seller also needs to inform the buyer when the product has been shipped. Both these Charge and Ship triggers are available as convenient buttons next to an order in the Merchant Centre. If you anticipate huge order volumes Google provides APIs to perform these actions automatically from your web application.

Google Checkout APIs

Google Checkout APIs provide developers with more power and control over the whole purchasing and payment process and the means to implement your own shopping cart and communicate with the Google Checkout cloud via web services.

The Checkout API deals with order information related to shopping-cart items and checkout flow support (shopping options and tax tables). A shopping cart can con-

---

[15] http://code.google.com/apis/checkout/developer/Google_Checkout_Shopping_Cart_Annotating_Pages.html
[16] http://code.google.com/apis/checkout/developer/index.html

tain multiple items. For each item, the information involved is generally similar to those supported by the CSS annotations we have seen earlier. However, the method of posting this information to Google Checkout is different depending on the chosen implementation option (HTML or XML).

There are two ways to implement the HTML option (the HTML in this sense refers to a POST action from a HTML form with appropriate fields, which can be simulated with PHP's cURL functions or Http extension). The first is by doing a form post with hidden form elements that stores items currently in a buyer's shopping cart. This way of creating a shopping cart is a little bit cumbersome as these hidden form elements have to be embedded across pages where we want to keep the shopping cart. With PHP, there are many better options to store the shopping cart in a buyer's session or otherwise. In this case, the other way to interact is via HTTP POST. PHP's cURL functions or PECL's HTTP extension can be used to perform these posts. For details on the parameters that have to be posted, check out the Google Checkout HTML API Developer's Guide. The POST request has to be authenticated with an Authorization_Key in the header. For PHP developers, this can be easily generated by doing `base64_encode(MERCHANT_ID:MERCHANT_KEY)`.

Besides the Checkout API, there are two other useful APIs. You can implement listeners (to order processing events from Google Checkout) on your internal order processing system with the Notification API. Google Checkout can send updates when orders have been received or when an order's status changes (e.g. when it is chargeable). Likewise, to authenticate notifications from Google Checkout, use `base64_decode()` to check the Authorization_Key. The Charge and Ship triggers that we introduced earlier can be sent via the Order Processing API instead of having to manually trigger these events on the Merchant Centre. The Custom Order Processing documentation in the Developer's Guide contains details on the implementation of these APIs.

The conceptual idea behind the XML API is similar to that of the HTML API but has XML sent via HTTP POST instead. The names of parameters in requests largely correlate to those used in the HTML API. The XML API also mandates the posting of digitally signed shopping carts, so it is ideal if this is a requirement for your application.

Google provides a sample PHP implementation detailing the various API usages on the Google Checkout Sample Code for PHP[17] page.

Paypal

Paypal is a comprehensive provider of payment services in the cloud. Its services are quite developer-centric, with helpful forums that detail some of the more intricate usage details left out by the API documentation. Several of its products are helpful when implementing applications with the use of the payment cloud. For example, the Permissions API allows developers to access customer information to build convenient services such as alerts. Adaptive Accounts allows developers to develop applications that create PayPal accounts on-the-fly as part of a check-out process, adding convenience for the end-user. The Virtual Terminal is basically a credit card terminal that lives in the cloud. PayFlow Pro is another powerful payment gateway that developers can use to process credit card transactions. Let's briefly walk through the process of submitting a transaction to PayFlow Pro. A basic set of transaction parameters are displayed below:

```
$transactionParams = array(
    'USER'      => PAYFLOWPRO_USER,
    'VENDOR'    => PAYFLOWPRO_VENDOR,
    'PARTNER'   => PAYFLOWPRO_PARTNER,
    'PWD'       => PAYFLOWPRO_PASSWORD,
    'TENDER'    => 'C',

    'TRXTYPE'   => 'S',
    'ACCT'      => $this->_request['cardNumber'],
    'EXPDATE'   => $this->_request['expiresOn'],
    'NAME'      => $this->_request['nameOnCard'],
    'AMT'       => ANNUAL_SUBSCRIPTION_RATE,
    'CURRENCY'  => ANNUAL_SUBSCRIPTION_CURRENCY,
    'COMMENT1'  => 'Annual payment for PictureMe subscription',
    'CVV2'      => $this->_request['csc'],
    'CLIENTIP'  => '0.0.0.0',
    'VERBOSITY' =>'MEDIUM'
);
```

---

[17] http://code.google.com/apis/checkout/samples/Google_Checkout_Sample_Code_PHP.html

This set of parameters creates a Sales transaction, indicated by TRXTYPE. The parameters submitted are mostly minimally required parameters. The PayFlow Pro Developer's Guide contains more comprehensive details on these and other optional parameters that can be used to customize the transaction. As for the request header, we'll need to create a unique ID where PHP's md5() function may come in handy. The actual submission of the request can then be achieved using PHP's cURL functions. See below.

```
$requestHeader = array(
   "X-VPS-REQUEST-ID: ". md5($this->_request['cardNumber'].time()),
   "X-VPS-CLIENT-TIMEOUT: 45",
);
$ch = curl_init();
curl_setopt($ch, CURLOPT_URL, PAYFLOWPRO_URL);
curl_setopt($ch, CURLOPT_HTTPHEADER, $requestHeader);
curl_setopt($ch, CURLOPT_RETURNTRANSFER, 1);
curl_setopt($ch, CURLOPT_TIMEOUT, 45);
curl_setopt($ch, CURLOPT_FOLLOWLOCATION, 0);
curl_setopt($ch, CURLOPT_SSL_VERIFYPEER, 0);
curl_setopt($ch, CURLOPT_POSTFIELDS, $this->_convertToString($transactionParams)
    );
curl_setopt($ch, CURLOPT_SSL_VERIFYHOST,  2);
curl_setopt($ch, CURLOPT_FORBID_REUSE, TRUE);
curl_setopt($ch, CURLOPT_POST, 1);
curl_setopt($ch, CURLOPT_VERBOSE, TRUE);
return curl_exec($ch);
```

We set CURLOPT_SSL_VERIFYPEER to 0 as HTTPS is used but we do not need to verify the peer's certificate. We submit the request as a POST. If you're interested in more details, check out the sample PictureMe source which has an example of how the whole payment process is managed from form submission to approval confirmation. There are also some examples of payment-related parameter validation methods using Zend_Validate.

CRM

CRM systems are the first function-specific enterprise applications that have made headway into transitioning to the cloud as Software-As-A-Service. Besides general-purpose applications such as Google Apps, the sales and customer service function within an organization is generally the most receptive of cloud-based applications, a real boost to adoption of cloud-based solutions given the importance of these functions in an organization's value chain, occupying a critical position within direct value-adding activities, as illustrated in Figure 7.4.

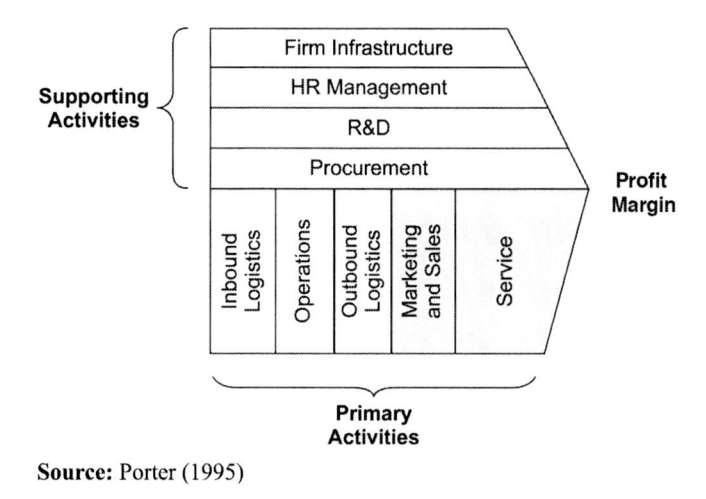

Source: Porter (1995)

Figure 7.4

The main reason for this phenomenon could be timing. Parallel to the growth of the cloud (which in essence is rooted in the growth of the internet) is the increase in the channels of communication between an organization and its customers. On top of the old ways of communicating via phone calls which in itself has increased in frequency, customer service departments are now confronted with new forms of customer communication such as online live-chats, Twitter messages, e-mails and other forms of aggregated internet-based B2B and B2C communication.

Couple these ways of communication with the significant decrease in the cost of operating these channels, the sales and customer service functions are faced with an increase in customer interaction workload and opportunities, and consequently an explosion of data and metrics to be strategically managed.

The good news is, as many customer-service departments have discovered, is that a good chunk of these interactions can be automated or outsourced, and the cloud-based CRM rises in importance in this new scenario with features that take advantage of high-volume internet-based interactions and remote access.

With regards to the CRM market as a whole, SAP and Oracle are leaders (22.5% and 16.1% market share respectively according to Gartner[18]) but the third placed Salesforce.com (10.6%) is the most cloud-focused, proudly exhorting its popular SaaS deployment model. Although SAP and Oracle are moving forward strong with "on-demand", Salesforce.com, bringing years of CRM expertise and domain knowledge from their wide customer-base to their SaaS offering, remains the most intriguing CRM option for PHP developers and managers because of its close alignment to a web-based philosophy and its foray into expanding its capabilities as a SaaS provider. In this section we will look into some of the features of the cloud-based web services and PHP toolkit that Salesforce.com provides.

Making Salesforce Easier with PHP

If your organization is using Salesforce.com and maintains a separate user database, which probably is the case, the administrator is going to find it a chore to have to create user accounts and manage rights on both systems. "Wouldn't it be nice to only have to manage users in our user database and extend rights to Salesforce.com functions from there?" will be the question ringing in the head of the administrator. Users themselves will also want seamless access to authorized Salesforce resources and functions via the company's portal without having to authenticate themselves again. These are scenarios where the Salesforce.com PHP toolkit and some cloud talking can come in handy, so let's take a look.

Connecting and Logging on to Salesforce.com

Salesforce uses a SOAP protocol for its web services, so we'll have to use a WSDL file to get access to the features it offers. There are various WSDL files for Salesforce depending on what services you need. These web services and their corresponding WSDLs are part of Force.com. Force.com is Salesforce's cloud-based application de-

---

[18] http://www.gartner.com/it/page.jsp?id=1074615

velopment platform. This platform can be used to develop unique web-applications but is popularly used to extend the functionalities of Salesforce's CRM. Integration with Salesforce.com is usually done through Force.com's web services API. In our first example, we will use the Partner WSDL file to interact with Salesforce.com. The partner WSDL file contains the Force.com object model that is generic to any organization. If you want to access your organization's custom fields and objects, then you'll need to use the Enterprise WSDL, which changes as custom fields and objects change.

Let's look at some sample code:

```
$wsdl = 'PATH_TO_SOAPCLIENT/partner.wsdl.xml';
    // If you're behind a proxy, you'll also need to instantiate a proxy settings
         object:
$proxy = new stdClass;
$proxy->host     = PROXY_URL;
$proxy->port     = PROXY_PORT;
$proxy->login    = PROXY_LOGIN;
$proxy->password = PROXY_PASSWORD;
```

We then instantiate an instance of `SforcePartnerClient`, create a connection and log in:

```
$partnerClient = new SforcePartnerClient();
$partnerClient->createConnection($wsdl, $proxy);
try {
    $partnerClient->login(USERNAME, PASSWORD_AND_TOKEN);
} catch (SoapFault $sf) {
    //...
}
```

As we are logging in via the API, a token is required as well. This token can be obtained from the Personal Setup section, which is accessible via conventional login to Salesforce via a browser. Append the token behind your password without any space. A `SoapFault` object is thrown if any exception is encountered.

Hint: `soap.wsdl_cache_enabled` is turned on by default, which is a good thing as you don't want PHP to retrieve the WSDL file every time it is used. However, this may cause problem in development especially if you're using new functions that are in the live WSDL but not in the cached WSDL file. It might just be more convenient to turn the WSDL cache off in your development environment during development, by calling:

```
ini_set('soap.wsdl_cache_enabled', 0);
```

Listing Profiles

A profile defines what a user can do in Salesforce. Before we create users, we need to get a list of profiles:

```
$profiles = $partnerClient->query('SELECT Id, Name from Profile');
```

Each user needs to be assigned a specific profile, this is done by placing the desired ProfileId value into the user creation object. Do note on the other hand that multiple users can have the same ProfileId, which means that they have the same kind and level of access to the functionalities within an organization's Salesforce application.

Creating a User

To create a user in Salesforce through the API, we first place relevant values for the user in an associative array. The ProfileId is obtained from the query we made earlier. We then create the SObject representing the user locally and pass it to the create method. We use array_map to apply htmlspecialchars() to convert any special characters into proper HTML entities. Here is the code for this:

```
$user = array(
    'Username'          => USERNAME,
    'Alias'             => ALIAS,
    'FirstName'         => FIRST_NAME,
    'LastName'          => LAST_NAME',
    'Email'             => EMAIL,
    'IsActive'          => 'true',
    'TimeZoneSidKey'    => 'Europe/London',
    'LocaleSidKey'      => 'en_GB',
    'EmailEncodingKey'  => 'ISO-8859-1',
    'LanguageLocaleKey' => 'en_GB',
```

```
    'ProfileId'        => PROFILE_ID,
);

$sObject = new SObject();
$sObject->fields = array_map('htmlspecialchars', $user);
$sObject->type = 'User';
$response = $partnerClient->create(array($sObject));
```

Disabling a User

It would seem convenient, but unfortunately `delete()` is not a valid call that can be applied to the User model. Instead of deleting a user, a user is disabled by updating the `IsActive` field to false, like we do here:

```
$updatedFields = array (
    'IsActive' => 'false'
);

$sObject1 = new SObject();
$sObject1->fields = $updatedFields;
$sObject1->type = 'User';
$sObject1->Id = USER_OBJECT_ID;

$response = $partnerClient->update(array($sObject1));
if ($response->success === true) {
    //...
}
```

Listing Users

To obtain a listing, or perform any query for that matter, we use the `query()` method. For example, if we want to obtain a list of users that are officially on Salesforce's records, we can do:

```
$response = $partnerClient->query(('SELECT Id, Name, ProfileId from User'));
```

Upserting a User

Since the record of a user cannot be deleted via the API, we may need to reactivate an inactive user if the case arises where the same username has to be used again. So instead of using create(), we can use 'upsert' ('update or insert') to either update the IsActive record of an existing user to true and change existing values associated to the username if the user already exists OR create the user if it does not. Here is an example:

```
$upsertFields = array(
    'Username' => USERNAME,
    'LastName' => NEW_LASTNAME,
    'FirstName' => NEW_FIRSTNAME,
    'IsActive' => 'true',
);

$sObject = new SObject();
$sObject->fields = $upsertFields;
$sObject->type = 'User';
$upsertResponse = $partnerClient->upsert("Username", array ($sObject));
```

It is more convenient to use upsert() in place of create() to be sure that we do not create additional data objects of a user if one already exist. Note how we use the Username field as an identifier for the object to upsert.

At this point, we are able to manage Salesforce.com users for an organization via PHP. This will allow us to synchronize records within an organization's user database to Salesforce.com's. Not all local users have to be reflected on Salesforce.com, just those that have the right to access Salesforce. What we have seen thus far provides us with the means to code something that manages users as we desire, making life much more convenient for the user administrator. We'll now look at making things convenient for the users themselves by allowing them to access Salesforce.com seamlessly from local systems without having to log in multiple times.

Creating an Authentication Web Service

Salesforce.com provides an alternative authentication mechanism that allows users to logon to Salesforce.com without specifying their username and password on the

Salesforce.com login page. Instead, Salesforce.com can pass authentication information to a delegated authentication web service that you'll need to implement.

Usually, this web service will be part of your SSO application. You will need to incorporate a web service that will be able to receive a SOAP request and return a response if the particular user has the correct credentials to access the organization's Salesforce.com. Details on the format of the requests and return are detailed in `AuthenticationService.wsdl` that can be downloaded from `Setup -> App Setup -> Develop -> API` in Salesforce. Here is the SoapServer implementation of this authentication service:

```
function Authenticate($credentials) {
    $rq = new stdClass();
    $user = new User($credentials->username, $credentials->password);
    if ($user->hasRight("external:salesforce")) {
        $rq->Authenticated = TRUE;
    } else {
        $rq->Authenticated = FALSE;
    }
    return $rq;
}

ini_set("soap.wsdl_cache_enabled", "0");
$server = new SoapServer("AuthenticationService.wsdl");
$server->addFunction("Authenticate");
$server->handle();
```

The `$user` object and the `hasRight()` call we perform on it is just an example. Your SSO should contain something similar. In essence, the credentials passed to the `Authenticate` method is checked against local SSO records. If the credentials are correct and this user has the appropriate rights to access Salesforce, then `TRUE` is returned. The `$credentials->password` passed does not need to be a password per se, it could be a token as well as long as the SSO component knows how to handle it. We'll take a look at this later.

Enabling Single Sign-On on Salesforce.com

Before we go further, you'll need to give Salesforce support a call in order to enable Single Sign-On for your organization. This is the only way to enable Single Sign-On at the time of writing. Once Salesforce support sends you an e-mail indicating that Single Sign-On (Delegated Administration) had been activated, you will then need to add the web service created earlier to the Delegated Gateway URL parameter within `Setup > Security Controls > Single Sign-On`. We'll also need to indicate profiles that can access Salesforce.com via Single Sign-On by enabling the `Is Single Sign-On enabled` field for the desired user profiles via the Salesforce.com site or via the API.

Access Salesforce.com Seamlessly from your Local Server

To make things easier for our users, users that are able to access Salesforce.com from your local system should be able to request access to Salesforce.com with a simple POST. This could be as simple as:

```
<form action='https://login.salesforce.com/' METHOD='POST' name='sso_login'>
<input type='hidden' name='un' runat='server' id='username' value= 'USERNAME'/>
<input type='hidden' name='pw' runat='server' id='token' value= 'TOKEN' />
<input type='hidden' name='logoutURL' runat='server' id='logoutURL' value= '' />
<input type='hidden' name='startURL' runat='server' id='startURL' value= '' />
<input type='hidden' name='ssoStartPage' runat='server' id='ssoStartPage' value=
      '' />
<input type='hidden' name='jse' value='0'>
<input type='hidden' name='rememberUn' value='1'>
<input type='submit' id='Login' name='Login' value='Login' />
</form>
```

A token is used in the form instead of a password in order not to expose the user's password unnecessarily. The access token is ideally generated by the local SSO service. Anyhow, the token should be made available to the authentication service that Salesforce.com will call so that it can be matched with the user before access is granted. Hence, the user can now access Salesforce.com with a single click triggering the form post instead of having to supply their credentials.

Conclusion

The features we have looked at are only a subset of the things that you can do on Salesforce.com. There are many more examples of the use of the PHP Toolkit[19] as well as a comprehensive reference[20] on the existing data model and available calls.

Maps

In previous sections, we have seen how the cloud helps in developing web-applications; going from back-end scalability and elasticity benefits from IaaS and PaaS clouds to more user focused features that are closer to the front-end of SaaS clouds. In this section, we shall go even further into the front-end; exploring the crème de la crème of front-end fanciness, the interactive universal map.

UI speaking, maps provide a more intuitive way to deliver proximity awareness than a line of location text. We'll not have to think very hard to get a feel of the possibilities of enhancing applications with this useful SaaS. There has been an explosive growth with the use of Maps SaaS, from one-off information pages, via business aggregators to mash-ups such as Ivo's experimental FrekFly[21]. There are several Map SaaS in the market, the most prominent few being Google Maps, Yahoo! Maps and Bing Maps. We will look into Google Maps in detail, mainly because of the popularity of its developer API but also because of its ease of use and innovative features.

Google Maps with PHP

The `GoogleMapAPI` class[22] is useful for dealing with Google Maps in PHP. Let's combine the use of this class and the `exif_read_data()` function in PHP to graphically display the location at which a photo is taken within PictureMe, our sample application. `exif_read_data()` can be used to obtain EXIF headers from a JPEG or TIFF file:

```
$exif = exif_read_data($this->_picture['url']);
```

---

[19] http://wiki.developerforce.com/index.php/PHP_Toolkit_13.0_Samples
[20] http://www.salesforce.com/us/developer/docs/api/index.htm
[21] http://www.frekfly.com/
[22] http://code.google.com/p/php-google-map-api/

Besides the fact that this will only work with JPEG or TIFF files, location information is only available on GPS-enabled digital cameras or mobile phones that support location storage within the EXIF headers. So, PictureMe will display location information only when it's possible. Anyway, it is easy to check for the presence of location information in PHP as exif_read_data returns an array of EXIF headers by default, and we only have to check if an array element with a GPSVersion key exists before proceeding:

```
if (!empty($exif['GPSVersion'])) {
    $picture['location'] = $this->showLocation($this->getLocation($exif));
}
```

The getLocation() is a method in PictureMe that does some mathematical manipulation upon the latitude and longitude information passed to it in the $exif array and returns an array consisting of the latitude and longitude in decimal format, which is used by showLocation() to create the necessary visualization for the represented location. This all happens in the domain of the GoogleMapAPI class.

The whole business of setting up the map visualization within PictureMe is rather easy, due to the simplicity of the GoogleMapAPI class and the Google Maps API. The setting up is as follows:

```
$this->_map = new GoogleMapAPI('map');
$this->_map->setAPIKey(GOOGLE_MAPS_API_KEY);
$this->_map->setWidth(720); //annoyingly not chainable
$this->_map->setHeight(200);
```

Once we have a properly constructed and configured _map object, any new location can be added by calling the addMarkerByCoords() method, passing in the longitude, latitude and the name of the picture. getMap() returns a snippet that displays the map <div> if JavaScript is enabled on the user's browser.

```
public function showLocation($location)
{
    $this->_map->addMarkerByCoords($location['Longitude'], $location['Latitude'],
        NULL, $this->getCurrentPictureName());
    return $this->_map->getMap();
}
```

Within the <head> tag of the view (index.php), we'll need to include the necessary Google Maps JavaScript and other JavaScript code to define the markers and create the GMap2 objects. Fortunately, GoogleMapAPI on the PHP end contains two convenient methods that we can call to do this to avoid any JavaScript-ing:

```
<head>
...
$header = $this->_map->getHeaderJS();
$map = $this->_map->getMapJS();
return $header.$map;
...
<body onload="onLoad()">
...
```

It is vital that the onLoad() function be called upon document load. Anyhow, PictureMe calls onLoad() and include the above two JavaScript snippets only if the photo currently displayed contains location information, to minimize page size. Figure 7.5 shows what a page with a photo that has location information within the EXIF headers will look like in PictureMe.

Storage

The final topic we will look at is that of cloud storage, which is not really a software as a service component but rather infrastructure as a service, but given that in this chapter we're looking at various components we can use in our own applications, it makes sense to end the book with a section on storage. It's not without a sense of Irony that we end with storage, given that many articles and presentations on clouds basically cover 'this is how to store data on Amazon S3' only, making it seem as if the cloud is nothing more than online data storage. We hope that we've shown you that there is a lot more to clouds than it might seem, and we hope that we've given you the info you need to start your own experimentations with cloud computing. With that said, let's get on with our final section. Given the abundance of how-to's on this subject, we won't give you any code this time, but a set of general guidelines that help you when working with storage services.

Generic cloud storage is an internet-accessible service that allows developers to store any amount of data objects of any kind. It is usually priced as a utility (like

148 ■ Working with Popular Cloud Software and Services

Figure 7.5

electricity), with a variable cost that may become lower as usage volume grows. For those intending to use cloud storage as part of their application or site, there are several important attributes to look out for:

Scalability

The paramount reason for using the storage cloud is on-demand scalability without having the need for capacity planning and hardware maintenance. A good cloud storage service provider should have a good track record that demonstrates their competency at managing this aspect of cloud storage.

Performance

The data transfer rate to store files on the cloud is generally much slower than dedicated local storage. This is due to the fact that data is transferred over the internet instead of over a controlled local network. Developers should realize this constraint and only use cloud storage for use-cases that are appropriate for the transfer rate.

Object Size

Most popular cloud storage services allow data objects of up to 5 GB in size.

Download Options

Usually HTTP should suffice but for larger distributions, BitTorrent[23] may be more cost-effective.

Security

An ACL and authentication mechanism to access data can be helpful, especially when data stored is private and user specific.

---

[23] http://docs.amazonwebservices.com/AmazonS3/latest/S3Torrent.html

Regional Optimization and Flexibility

If there is a tendency for some of your objects to be accessed within a certain region, then you should check that the cloud storage service allows you to place it within a cloud location that is physically closer to that region. For example, video dramas that have more European audiences should obviously be placed within Europe. Regional flexibility may also be important to comply with regulatory requirements.

Reliability

Be sure to check if reliability levels are formalized by a Service Level Agreement and that the service level fits your requirement and compensation expectations. It is also a good idea to see if the storage service provider has a good backup and redundancy policy in place.

Cost-Efficiency

There is heavy competition within the cloud storage market, so storage, transfer rate and requests are almost priced like undifferentiated commodity between the competing providers. However, do take into consideration that some vendors may charge different prices for different storage regions and for extra functionalities.

The following are some of the more popular cloud storage service providers. All of these providers have web services that can be accessed via PHP using the appropriate REST or SOAP tools. To get a feel of how to use cloud storage with PHP, take a look at section 4.1.1.

Amazon Simple Storage Service (S3)

S3 is arguably the most popular cloud storage service on the internet. It rides on the same cloud that Amazon uses to run its own global network of sites. It integrates very well with other Amazon Web Services such as Elastic MapReduce (EMR) and Elastic Compute Cloud (EC2) and can be geographically optimized with CloudFront.

Rackspace Cloud Files

From the company with a strong legacy in IT infrastructure hosting comes a strong competitor to S3. Its Content Delivery Network is included free (CloudFront is a chargeable service at time of writing) and is run by Limelight Networks, the specialists in CDNs that includes Microsoft Xbox, Netflix and MSNBC as some of their customers. Similarly, Cloud Files will also be appealing to companies that run their applications on Rackspace Cloud Servers as data transfer between server and storage will be faster within the same Rackspace network.

Nirvanix Storage Delivery Network

The most outstanding feature of Nirvanix is the support of file size of up to 256 GB versus the 5GB maximum of most other popular cloud storage service providers. It is also strong on the security and reliability front and is openly explicit on their effort and competence in these aspects. Nirvanix's CloudNAS allows cloud storage to be mounted as a storage device and hence access to cloud storage without using a web services API.

The Planet's Storage Cloud

This service is bundled free (up to 10GB) for The Planet's server hosting customers, where it is most suitably used to achieve the performance and flexibility of a NAS (Network Attached Storage). Also supports Nirvanix's CloudNAS.

EMC Atmos Online Storage Service

This cloud storage service is based on Atmos, EMC's offering to those wishing to build their own cloud. Atmos includes features such as policy-based information management and object meta data definition for those that require fine-grained control over data storage location and distribution within the cloud.

Conclusion

A thorough comparison of these offerings can fill up a whole book and is subject to change and enhancement as competition heats up. In making decisions as to which cloud to go for, we hope you are able to use some of the discussion here to identify what to look out for, versus your development needs and business constraints. It also may be worth considering a higher level cloud storage abstraction, such as the SimpleCloud Storage Service API so that you can switch between services with less hassle. Be wary though of specialized features which may not be covered by the abstraction.